ECDL

Advanced Spreadsheets

ECDL

Advanced Spreadsheets

Sharon Murphy
and Paul Holden

ECDL Approved Courseware
Syllabus Version 3.0

Prentice
Hall

An imprint of Pearson Education

London · Boston · Indianapolis · New York · Mexico City · Toronto · Sydney · Tokyo · Singapore
Hong Kong · Cape Town · New Delhi · Madrid · Paris · Milan · Amsterdam · Munich · Milan · Stockholm

PEARSON EDUCATION LIMITED

Head Office:
Edinburgh Gate
Harlow CM20 2JE
Tel: +44 (0)1279 623623
Fax: +44 (0)1279 431059

London Office:
128 Long Acre
London WC2E 9AN
Tel: +44 (0)20 7447 2000
Fax: +44 (0)20 7240 5771

Website: www.it-minds.com

First published in Great Britain in 2002

© Rédacteurs Limited 2002

ISBN 0-130-98983-5

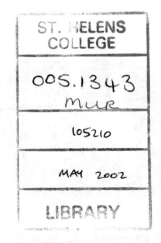

British Library Cataloguing in Publication Data
A CIP catalogue record for this book can be obtained from the British Library.

'European Computer Driving Licence' and ECDL and Stars device are registered trademarks of the European Computer Driving Licence Foundation Limited in Ireland and other countries. Rédacteurs Limited is an independent entity from the European Computer Driving Licence Foundation Limited, and is not affiliated with the European Computer Driving Licence Foundation in any manner.

ECDL Advanced Spreadsheets may be used in assisting students to prepare for a European Computer Driving Licence (Advanced) Examination. None of the European Computer Driving Licence Foundation Limited, Rédacteurs Limited or the publisher warrants that the use of *ECDL Advanced Spreadsheets* will ensure passing the relevant examination.

Use of the ECDL-F approved courseware Logo on this product signifies that it has been independently reviewed and approved in complying with the following standards:

Acceptable coverage of all courseware content related to ECDL Syllabus (Advanced) Version 1.0. This courseware has not been reviewed for technical accuracy and does not guarantee that the end user will pass the associated ECDL (Advanced) Examinations. Any and all assessment tests and/or performance-based exercises contained in *ECDL Advanced Spreadsheets* relate solely to this book and do not constitute, or imply, certification by the European Driving Licence Foundation in respect of any ECDL (Advanced) Examinations. For details on sitting ECDL examinations in your country, please contact the local ECDL licensee or visit the European Computer Driving Licence Foundation Limited website at www.ecdl.com.

References to the European Computer Driving Licence (ECDL) include the International Computer Driving Licence (ICDL).

ECDL Foundation Syllabus (Advanced) Version 1.0 is published as the official syllabus for use within the European Computer Driving Licence (ECDL) and International Computer Driving licence (ICDL) certification programmes.

Rédacteurs Limited is at www.redact.ie

10 9 8 7 6 5 4 3 2 1

Typeset by Pantek Arts Ltd, Maidstone, Kent.
Printed and bound in Great Britain by Ashford Colour Press, Gosport, Hampshire.

The publishers' policy is to use paper manufactured from sustainable forests.

Preface

What is ECDL?

ECDL, or the European Computer Driving Licence, is an internationally recognized qualification in information technology skills. It is accepted by businesses internationally as a verification of competence and proficiency in computer skills.

The ECDL syllabus is neither operating system nor software specific.

For more information about ECDL, and to see the syllabus for *ECDL Module 4, Spreadsheets, Advanced Level*, visit the official ECDL website at www.ecdl.com.

About this book

This book covers the ECDL Advanced Spreadsheets syllabus Version 1.0, using Excel 2000 to complete all the required tasks. It is assumed that you have already completed the spreadsheets module of ECDL 3 using Excel, or you have an equivalent knowledge of the product.

The chapters in this book are intended to be read sequentially. Each chapter assumes that you have read and understood the information in the preceding chapters.

Each exercise in the book builds on the results of previous exercises. The exercises should be completed in order.

Additional exercises, labelled *Over to you*, have been posed for you to complete. These exercises provide limited guidance as to how to go about performing the tasks, since you should have learned what you need in the preceding exercises. Some of these exercises are marked as mandatory and others as optional. The changes you make in the mandatory exercises are used in later exercises in the book.

Hardware and software requirements

Your PC should meet the following specifications:

- Pentium 75 MHz or higher processor.
- Windows 95 or later.
- 22 MB RAM if you are running Excel on Windows 95 or 98, or 36 MB RAM on later versions of Windows.
- CD-ROM drive.
- 500 KB of free space on your hard disk.
- Excel 2000.
- Microsoft Query.
- Word 2000.

Typographic conventions

The following typographic conventions are used in this book:

Bold text is used to denote command names, button names, menu names, the names of tabs in dialog boxes, and keyboard keys.

Italicized text is used to denote cross-references within the book, as well as field names, options in drop-down lists and list boxes, dialog box names, areas in dialog boxes, toolbars, cells in spreadsheets, and text entered in cells and fields.

ARIAL NARROW TEXT is used to denote the names of folders and files, and, when italicized, the names of worksheets in Excel workbooks.

Contents

Chapter 4: Sorting data in a spreadsheet   29

Chapter 5: Naming cells and adding comments   37

Chapter 6: Using Paste Special   45

Chapter 7: Summarizing data using PivotTables   55

Chapter 8: Linking data in spreadsheets   65

Chapter 9: Formatting your spreadsheets   73

Chapter 12: Customizing charts   103

Chapter 13: Using statistical and database functions   117

Chapter 14: Using financial functions   125

Chapter 15: Using text and date functions   *133*

Chapter 16: Using logical functions   *139*

Chapter 17: Using data tables and scenarios   *147*

Chapter 18: Auditing your spreadsheets   157

Chapter 19: Sharing and protecting your spreadsheets   165

In conclusion   173

Index   175

1 Introduction

The case study

The exercises in this book relate to the spreadsheets used by a fictitious company, Murphy's Flatpack Furniture, or MFPF.

MFPF is a family-run business, producing a range of flatpack furniture. The current range includes five indoor pieces (bed, wardrobe, chest of drawers, coffee table and kitchen organizer), and two outdoor pieces (garden chair and garden table).

MFPF sells furniture to six retailers: three in Cullenstown, where MFPF is based, and three in neighbouring villages.

Mr and Mrs Murphy are not salaried, but they retain any profits made by the business. Their daughter works in the warehouse and receives a monthly salary.

Regular business expenses are materials, warehouse rental, petrol, electricity and telephone.

You have just been hired as a bookkeeper for the business. Your duties include looking after invoices, maintaining records on the financial transactions of the business, and producing reports, summaries and forecasts when requested.

The CD

The CD supplied with this book contains the following files:

- DELIVERY_COSTS.TXT – a delimited text file that lists the road distance to each customer and the delivery charge applied to their orders.
- INVOICE_MFPF.XLT – an Excel template for sales invoices.
- LETTER.DOC – the start of a letter to the local bank manager, in relation to a business loan.
- LOGO.GIF – MFPF's company logo.
- MFPF_FINANCE.XLS – the start of a spreadsheet used to track the business's annual incomings, outgoings and profits.

- MFPF_ORD.MDB – an Access database containing details of MFPF's customers and all the orders they placed in 2000.
- OUTGOING.TXT – a delimited text file that lists the monthly costs of regular business expenses.
- PASTE_SPECIAL.XLS – a spreadsheet containing an assortment of miscellaneous information.
- PRICES.TXT – a delimited text file listing the costs of materials for each furniture type produced, and the price at which the finished products are sold.

You will use these files when completing the exercises in the book.

Before you start

Before you begin working through the exercises in this book, you will need to copy the files from the CD to your computer.

Copying files from the CD

In the following exercise, you will copy the INVOICE_MFPF.XLT template to Excel's templates folder, then create a working folder to which you will copy the remainder of the files from the CD.

Exercise 1.1: Copying files from the CD to your computer

1) Copy the Excel template INVOICE_MFPF.XLT from the CD to the following folder:
Application Data\Microsoft\Templates
Where this folder is located will depend on how your computer has been set up.

2) Create a folder called ECDL_EXCEL anywhere on your computer. This will be your working folder for the exercises in this book.

3) Copy all the other files from the disk to the ECDL_EXCEL folder.

Turning off adaptive menus

Excel's adaptive menus show the commands you have used most recently first. Since the exercises in this book require less commonly used commands, you should turn off adaptive menus before you start.

Exercise 1.2: Turning off adaptive menus

1)   Start Excel.

2)   Select **View | Toolbars | Customize** ... .
     The *Customize* dialog box opens.

3)   Click the **Options** tab.

4)   Uncheck the box beside *Menus show recently used commands first*
     and click **Close**.

2

Using Templates in Excel

In this chapter

Every time you create a new spreadsheet in Excel, you base it on a template.

In this chapter you will learn about templates in Excel: what they are, what information they contain, and how to use them. You will also learn how to edit templates, and how to create templates of your own.

New skills

At the end of this chapter you should be able to:

- Explain what a template is
- Explain why you would want to use a template
- Give examples of the type of information that can be stored in a template
- Find Excel templates on your PC
- Create spreadsheets from templates
- Create and edit templates

New words

At the end of this chapter you should be able to explain the following terms:

- Template
- Boilerplate text

Creating spreadsheets from templates

Every time you create a new spreadsheet in Excel, you use a template that defines the default settings and content for the spreadsheet.

Template

In Excel, a template is a type of spreadsheet that contains default information and settings, and is used to create new spreadsheets with the same look and feel. Excel templates have the file extension .xlt.

Even the 'empty' workbook that opens by default when you start Excel is based on a template. The template contains no text or numeric data, but it does have default layout and style content.

Start Excel and have a closer look at the default workbook that opens.

Normally, the default workbook contains three worksheets. (The default may have been changed on your computer.) Each worksheet has 256 columns and 65,536 rows. Every column has a standard width; every row has a standard height. The font in every cell is Arial 10 point. All of this is defined by the default template.

Most templates you use in Excel contain default text, such as row and column labels, which is included in every new spreadsheet generated from the template. This text is known as boilerplate text.

Boilerplate text

Default text included in a template is called boilerplate text. It is added to every spreadsheet created from that template.

Templates can also contain layout and style formatting, numbers, formulae, macros, charts and any other type of information or setting that can be added to a spreadsheet in Excel.

Using a template to generate a particular type of spreadsheet that you use regularly can save you a lot of time and effort. Only the case-specific data will need to be added each time.

Mr Murphy has given you your first task for Murphy's Flatpack Furniture. He wants you to issue an invoice to a customer, using Excel. The invoice should indicate who has issued it and when, who it was issued to, and what goods were ordered and how much they cost. MFPF will keep an electronic copy of the invoice for its own records and print out a copy to send to the customer.

To create the invoice, you could start with the default workbook and add labels and numbers for the required details, and then apply formatting before printing it and sending it to the customer. Fortunately, though, there's an invoice template available with all the default information already there.

> **Note:** If you didn't complete *Exercise 1.1* on page 2 you should go back and do it now. The exercises use files supplied on the disk that comes with the book. These files must be in specific locations before you start.

Exercise 2.1: Creating a spreadsheet from a template

1) Start Excel, if it is not already open.

2) Select **File | New ...**
    The *New* dialog box opens.

3) Click the **General** tab.
    A list of available templates is shown.

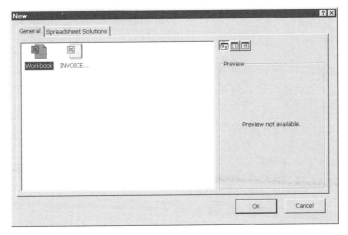

4) Select INVOICE_MFPF.XLT and click **OK**.
    A new spreadsheet opens.
    This spreadsheet contains all the default information and settings defined by the template.
    To write an invoice, you just need to fill in the blanks.

Save
button

5) Select **File | Save**, or click the **Save** button on the *Standard* toolbar. The *Save As* dialog box opens.

6) Name the spreadsheet INVOICE1.XLS, and save it in your working folder, ECDL_EXCEL.

Over to you: optional

Next, you will look at some more templates.

The *New* dialog box lists all the templates available on your computer. The **Spreadsheet Solutions** tab contains four templates that have been provided by Microsoft. All other templates are shown on the **General** tab. *Workbook* is the default template we saw earlier.

- Open the other templates on your computer and see what information and settings they contain. Try to think of other spreadsheet templates you might find useful.

Creating templates

You can create a new template by adding the default information and settings you want in the template to a spreadsheet, and then saving the spreadsheet as a template using **File | Save as ...** .

When you save a spreadsheet as a template, Excel automatically changes the file extension to .XLT and opens the correct folder for saving Excel templates.

You can add templates to the **General** tab of the *New* dialog box by putting Excel template files in any of these folders:

- C:\<OS>\PROFILES\<USERNAME>\APPLICATIONDATA\MICROSOFT\ TEMPLATES
- C:\<OS>\PROFILES\<USERNAME>\APPLICATIONDATA\MICROSOFT\ EXCEL\XLSTART
- The folder specified in the *Default file location* field on the **General** tab of the dialog box opened by selecting **Tools | Options ...** .

In the first two of these, <OS> should be replaced by the name of the operating system you are running, for example WINNT, and <USERNAME> should be replaced by your username on the computer.

Editing templates

There are two ways to edit an existing template:

- Select **File | Open ...** , locate the template, edit it directly, and save your results.

  – or –

- Select **File | New ...** , create a new spreadsheet based on the template, make changes to the spreadsheet, then save it as a template, using the name of the existing template.

The second option is preferable, because if you decide at any point that you are not happy with your changes, you still have the original template and have not lost any work.

Editing a template

There are some problems with the invoice template you used earlier. There is a typo in the company name on the first page, and despite a request that the invoice be paid within 28 days there is nowhere to indicate what date it was issued!

In the following exercise, you will create a spreadsheet from the invoice template, edit the spreadsheet to fix these problems and make some other formatting changes, and then save it as a template, replacing the original INVOICE_MFPF.XLT.

Exercise 2.2: Editing a template

1) Create a new spreadsheet based on the invoice template.

2) Select **File | Save**, or click the **Save** button on the *Standard* toolbar.

3) Name your file INVOICE_MFPF.XLS and save it in the ECDL_EXCEL folder.

4) Make the following changes to the spreadsheet:

   - On the **Customer Invoice** worksheet, fix the typo in the spelling of *Murphy*.

   - Increase the font size for the invoice total in cell *F21* to 12 point.

   - Decrease the font size for the list of goods in cell range *B11:B19* to 10 point.

   - The invoice should be paid within 28 days, but the issue date is not indicated anywhere. Enter the label *Date:* in cell *E5*, and format it as bold italic.

5) Save your workbook when you are done.

6) Select **File | Save as ...** , and select *Template (*.xlt)* from the *Save as type* drop-down list.
   Excel changes the file extension and automatically opens the TEMPLATES folder.

7) Select the existing INVOICE_MFPF.XLT to replace it, and click **Save**.
   A dialog box appears, asking you to confirm that you want to replace the existing INVOICE_MFPF.XLT.

8) Click **Yes**.

Congratulations! You just saved your first template. Just think about how much time and energy you will save in the future when you have created templates for all of the spreadsheets you use regularly.

Over to you: optional

To see that your changes are now part of the invoice template, you will create a new spreadsheet based on the template.

- Create a new spreadsheet based on INVOICE_MFPF.XLT. Check that the changes you made in *Exercise 2.2* on page 10 are now part of the default information in the template. Close Excel when you are finished.

Chapter summary

In Excel, a template is a type of spreadsheet that contains default information and settings, and is used to create new spreadsheets with the same look and feel. Excel templates have the file extension .xlt.

Templates can contain any type of information or setting that can be added to a spreadsheet in Excel, including text, layout and style formatting, numbers, formulae, macros and charts.

Default text included in a template is called boilerplate text. It is added to every spreadsheet created from that template.

3

Importing Data into a Spreadsheet

In this chapter

From time to time, you may find that you want to reuse all or same of the data from another source in an Excel spreadsheet.

For example, you might want to reuse a list of staff members from a telephone list as row labels in a worksheet where you will calculate your annual salary budget. Or you might want to include petty cash records from a database in your expenses calculations.

Excel's data import facility allows you to import all or part of the data in a delimited text file or a database into a spreadsheet. In this chapter you will learn how to import data from delimited text files and from an Access database into Excel.

New skills

At the end of this chapter you should be able to:

- Import data from delimited text files
- Import data from a database using a query
- Run a saved database query
- Edit a database query
- Add filter and sort requirements to a database query

New words

At the end of this chapter you should be able to explain the following terms:

- Delimited text file
- Text qualifier
- Query
- Criteria
- Filter

Importing data from an external source

In ECDL 3 you imported objects created in other programs into Excel spreadsheets. These objects included images and text files.

You can also choose to import text from an external source and include it in the cells of an Excel spreadsheet. These data can then be formatted, manipulated and used in formulae, just like any other data in Excel.

Refresh Data button

When you import data from an external source, Excel remembers which file or database you imported your data from, and the setting you used to import it. If the data in the source file change, you can update the imported data in Excel by selecting the imported data, and then selecting **Data | Refresh Data** or clicking the **Refresh Data** button on the *External Data* toolbar.

If you cannot see the *External Data* toolbar, you can turn it on by selecting **View | Toolbars | External Data**.

Importing data from text files

When you import data from a text file, the text file will usually be formatted in rows and columns. You can use Excel's *Text Import Wizard* to specify how the data have been formatted, so that you can preserve the row and column structure when you import the data into Excel.

Structured text files

When importing structured text files, Excel treats each new line as a row. Excel recognizes two different ways that columns can be represented:

- The columns can be *delimited*, which means that a particular character or set of characters is used to indicate where one column stops and the next begins.
- The columns can be structured with a *fixed width*, which means that a number of tabs and spaces, or a combination of the two, is used to make all the entries in a column line up.

Text qualifiers

If any of the data elements in your delimited text file contain the character that has been used as a delimiter, you can use a text qualifier to mark the beginning and end of the data element. The *Text Import Wizard* ignores any delimiter characters that appear between a pair of text qualifiers.

Importing delimited text files

Mrs Murphy has asked you to import data about MFPF's business expenses from three delimited text files into spreadsheets, where the data can be used in calculations of monthly running costs.

The three files are:

- OUTGOING.TXT, which is space-delimited and shows the regular expenses incurred by the business every month.
- PRICES.TXT, which is tab-delimited and shows the cost of the materials for each type of furniture produced by the business, and the wholesale price for which they are sold.
- DELIVERY_COSTS.TXT, which is comma-delimited and shows the distance to each customer's premises, and the delivery charge for each order.

Each file uses double quotation marks as text qualifiers.

In the next exercise, you will import the first of these files into the MFPF_FINANCE.XLS spreadsheet.

Exercise 3.1: Importing a space-delimited text file

1) Open the spreadsheet MFPF_FINANCE.XLS.

2) Select **Data | Get External Data | Import Text File ...** .
    The *Import Text File* dialog box opens.

3) Select outgoing.txt in your working folder and click **Import**.
    The *Text Import Wizard* opens.

4) Indicate that your data are *Delimited*, and that you want to *Start import at row 1*.
    Click **Next**.

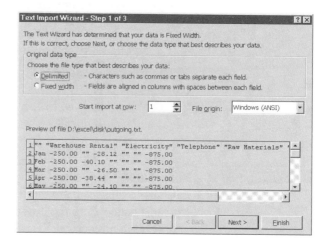

5) The file you are importing is space-delimited, so in the *Delimiters* area on the dialog box that now appears, check the box beside *Space*.

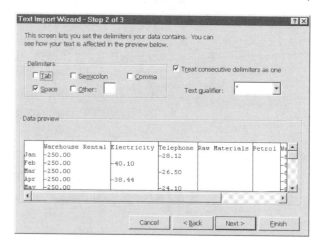

In the *Text qualifier* field, select the double quotation mark.
Click **Next**.

6) In the *Column data format* area, you can specify a format for the column selected in the *Data preview* area, or select *Do not import column* to skip the column when importing.

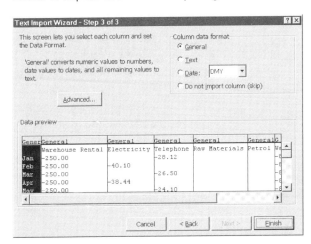

To select a column, click anywhere in it in the *Data preview* area of the dialog box.
In this case, you will import all the columns with a *General* format.
Click **Finish**.
The *Import Data* dialog box opens.

7) Specify that you want to add the data to the *OUTGOING* worksheet, in the cell range starting in cell *A1*.
Either enter the details below manually, or open the *OUTGOING* worksheet and click in cell *A1* to automatically add the correct cell reference to the *Existing worksheet* field of the *Import Data* dialog box.

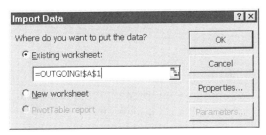

Click **OK**.
The data from the text file are added to the *OUTGOING* worksheet.

8) Save your workbook.

Well done! You have just imported a year's worth of expenses information from a space-delimited text file into a spreadsheet in a matter of minutes.

Next, you will import the other two delimited text files into other worksheets.

- Import the data from PRICES.TXT into MFPF_FINANCE.XLS. Add the data in a cell range starting at cell *A15* on the *SALES TOTALS* worksheet. The first row in PRICES.TXT contains the column titles already present on this worksheet, so you do not need to include them: start your import at row *2*. Import all columns with a general format. When you are done, save and close the workbook.

- Create a new workbook called DELIVERIES.XLS based on the default template. Rename one of the worksheets *CHARGES* and import DELIVERY_COSTS.TXT into it. When you are done, save and close the workbook.

Querying a database from Excel

You have successfully imported data from a variety of delimited text files. Next, you will learn how to import data from a database.

To import data from a database, you create a query that specifies the information you want. Then you run the query, and put the results in your Excel spreadsheet.

Query
A query is a set of rules that specifies what records, or parts of records, to retrieve from a database, and how to display those data.

Creating a simple query

The Access database MFPF_ORD.MDB contains contact information for each of Murphy's Flatpack Furniture's customers, and details of their orders for the year 2000.

You have been asked to import from the database only those columns that indicate the date of an order, the company that made the order, the town it is based in, and how many units of each type of furniture it ordered.

In the next exercise, you will create a simple query to import the specified columns from MFPF_ORD.MDB. You will also save the query you create so that you can run it again later.

Exercise 3.2: Creating a simple database query in Excel

1) Create a new workbook called MFPF_ORD.XLS, based on the default template, and rename the first worksheet *COMPLETE*.

2) Select **Data | Get External Data | New Database Query ...** .
   The *Choose Data Source* dialog box opens.

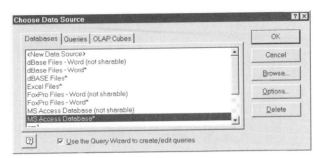

3) Select *MS Access Database** from the list of databases.
   Make sure the box beside *Use the Query Wizard to create/edit queries* is checked, then click **OK**.
   The *Select Database* dialog box opens.

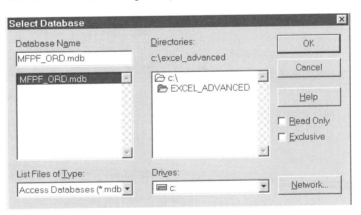

4) Select the MFPF_ORD.MDB database in your working folder.
   If your working folder is not on the C drive, you will need to select the correct drive in the *Drives* field first.
   Click **OK**.

The *Query Wizard – Choose Columns* dialog box opens.

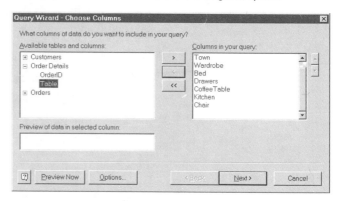

5) Select the following columns in this order:

- *OrderDate* from the *Orders* table.

- *CompanyName* and *Town* from the *Customers* table.

- *Wardrobe*, *Bed*, *Drawers*, *CoffeeTable*, *Kitchen*, *Chair* and *Table* from the *Order Details* table.

Keep clicking **Next** until you get to the *Query Wizard – Finish* dialog box.

6) Select **Save Query ...** .
The *Save As* dialog box opens.

7) Name the query *MFPF_Q1.DQY* and click **Save**.

8) Select *Return Data to Microsoft Excel* and click **Finish**.
The *Returning External Data to Microsoft Excel* dialog box opens.

9) Specify that you want to put the data in the cell range beginning in cell *A1* on the *COMPLETE* worksheet, and click **OK**.

10) Save your workbook.

Over to you: mandatory

Next, you will create a query to retrieve the columns that indicate the order date and company name for each order placed. These details will be used later to calculate delivery charges and petrol costs for each order.

- Open DELIVERIES.XLS and create a query that retrieves from MFPF_ORD.MDB the following columns (in order): *DeliveryDate* and *CompanyName* from the *Orders* table. Add the results to a new worksheet. Name the new worksheet *DELIVERIES*.

When you are done, save and close the workbook.

Chapter 3: Importing Data into a Spreadsheet

Using filter and sort in a database query

When you import data from delimited text files, you choose which columns to include, and at which row to start the import.

When you import data from a database, you have much more control over which rows (or records) to include. You can specify a set of criteria that the records you import should satisfy.

> **Criteria**
>
> *Criteria are rules that specify what records are imported, based on the value in a particular field.*

For example, you could use criteria to indicate that the value in a particular field must match exactly a specified value.

Criteria are combined together to create a filter.

> **Filter**
>
> *A filter limits the records imported from a database to those that satisfy a set of criteria.*

You can even sort the records before importing them into your spreadsheet.

Running a saved query

Mrs Murphy has asked you to add two more worksheets to the MFPF_ORD.XLS workbook. The first should show order details for outdoor furniture (garden chairs and garden tables). The second should show details for indoor furniture (bed, wardrobe, chest of drawers, coffee table and kitchen organizer).

Additionally, she only wants to see the records for sales to customers in Cullenstown on each of these sheets.

In the next exercise, you will run the query you saved earlier to import order records into a new worksheet.

Exercise 3.3: Running a saved query

1) Open MFPF_ORD.XLS, and name one of the empty worksheets *INDOOR*.

2) Select **Data | Get External Data | Run Saved Query ... .**
   The *Run Query* dialog box opens.

3) Select *MFPF_Q1.DQY* (the query you saved earlier) and click **Get Data**.
   The *Returning External Data to Microsoft Excel* dialog box opens.

4) Specify that you want to put the data in the cell range beginning in cell *A1* on the *INDOOR* worksheet and click **OK**.

5) Save your workbook.

The *INDOOR* worksheet now contains the same information you imported into the *COMPLETE* worksheet when you first created and ran the MFPF_Q1.DQY query.

Editing queries

In the next exercise, you will edit the query to import information about sales of indoor furniture only. You will also add a filter so that only records relating to customers in Cullenstown are imported. Finally, just to make the results easier to read, you will sort the records in reverse chronological order, so that the most recent orders appear first.

> **Note:** You will not save the changes you make to the query, so the next time you run it, the results will be unfiltered and unsorted, as before.

Exercise 3.4: Editing a query

Edit Query ...
button

1) Select any cell in the range that contains the imported data, and select **Data | Get External Data | Edit Query ...** , or click the **Edit Query ...** button on the *External Data* toolbar.
   If you cannot see the *External Data* toolbar, open it by selecting **View | Toolbars | External Data**.

2) Remove the columns for the sales of *Chairs* and *Tables*.
   Click **Next**.

The *Query Wizard – Filter Data* dialog box opens.

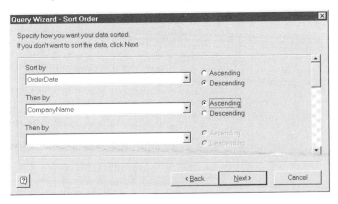

3) In this dialog box, you will create a filter to limit the records returned by the query to those related to orders from customers in Cullenstown.
Select *Town* in the *Column to filter* list box, then select *equals* and *Cullenstown* in the *Only include rows where* area.
This is a criterion in your filter.
You could add any number of other criteria to *Town* and other columns in this dialog box, if you wanted to.
You can combine the criteria for a single column using either logical AND or logical OR.
The filter requirements for different columns are combined using logical AND. This means that for a record to get through the filter, it should satisfy the filter requirements you set for each column.

4) Click **Next**.
The *Query Wizard – Sort Order* dialog box opens.

5) Sort by *OrderDate Descending* to see the most recent sales first. Then select *CompanyName Ascending*, so that if more than one sale was made on the same date, the sales for that date will be listed alphabetically by customer.
Click **Next**.

6) Select *Return Data to Microsoft Excel* and click **Finish**.

7) Save your workbook.

Well done! You've accomplished a lot this time. You have learned how to run a saved query, how to edit that query, and how to use filter and sort when querying.

Over to you: mandatory

Next, you will filter the results from the saved query MFPF_Q1.DQY to show results for outdoor furniture, filtered and sorted in the same way.

- In the MFPF_ORD.XLS workbook, create a worksheet called *OUTDOOR*.

- Run the saved query MFPF_Q1.DQY and put the results on the *OUTDOOR* worksheet, starting in cell *A1*.

- Edit the query to show records for outdoor furniture sold in Cullenstown only, sorted in reverse chronological order.

- Save your workbook.

Advanced querying

Looking at the query results on the *INDOOR* and *OUTDOOR* worksheets, you can see that there are rows where none of the specified types of furniture were sold. These records are not really of any interest, but there is no way to filter them out using the *Query Wizard*.

Although you can combine the criteria for a given column using logical AND or logical OR, the sets of criteria for different columns are always combined using logical AND in the *Query Wizard*.

For example, you could create a filter to find orders where one or more of every furniture type was ordered, but not one where one or more of any one furniture type was ordered. To do that, you would need to be able to combine column filters using logical OR.

You can edit your query in Microsoft Query, instead of in the *Query Wizard*, to set more complex filters, using both logical AND and logical OR to combine all of your criteria, regardless of which columns they refer to.

Filters in Microsoft Query

In Microsoft Query, criteria are combined using logical AND and logical OR to create a set of distinct filter requirements.

Here is an example of how a set of filter requirements is represented in Microsoft Query:

Criteria consist of *Criteria Fields* and *Values*. If a *Value* cell is left blank, then any value for the corresponding *Criteria Field* is acceptable.

Each row represents a single filter requirement, where the criteria are combined using logical AND.

The individual rows are combined using logical OR.

So, for a record to get through the filter, it must satisfy all of the criteria in any one row.

In the example shown, a record will get through the filter if it is an order from *Joe's Hardware* AND at least one *Bed* was ordered, OR if it is an order from *Mullens* AND at least two *Coffee Tables* were ordered. No other records will get through.

Before you start to define a filter in Microsoft Query, you should be clear *exactly* what your filter requirements are, and how they relate to each other.

Creating an advanced filter

You want to filter out the records on the *INDOOR* and *OUTDOOR* worksheets of MFPF_ORD.XLS where no furniture was ordered. Remember that Mrs Murphy asked only to see records for customers in Cullenstown.

The individual filter requirements you will need to create are:

- The customer is from Cullenstown AND at least one bed was ordered
  OR

- The customer is from Cullenstown AND at least one wardrobe was ordered
  OR

- etc.

In the next exercise, you will use Microsoft Query to create an advanced query filter that finds records where at least one piece of indoor furniture was ordered by a shop in Cullenstown.

Exercise 3.5: Using advanced filtering in Microsoft Query

1) Open MFPF_ORD.XLS and go to the *INDOOR* worksheet.

2) Select any cell in the query results, and select **Data | Get External Data | Edit Query ...** , or click the **Edit Query ...** button on the *External Data* toolbar.
   The *Query Wizard* opens.

3) Click **Cancel**.
   A dialog box opens asking you if you would like to continue editing the query in Microsoft Query.

4) Click **Yes**.
   Microsoft Query opens.

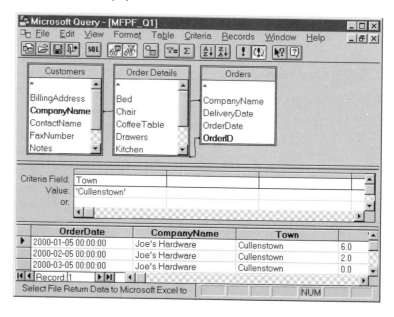

5) Select **Criteria | Remove All Criteria** to delete the filter you set earlier for the *Town* column area, before you add new filter rules.

6) You could add your criteria by typing directly in the *Criteria Field* and *Value* cells, but instead you will use the *Add Criteria* dialog box. Select **Criteria | Add Criteria ...** .
The *Add Criteria* dialog box appears.

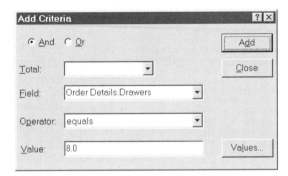

7) Add the following criteria to your filter in order, clicking **Add** after specifying each one:

And/Or	Field	Operator	Value
	Order Details.Bed	Is greater than	*0*
Or	Order Details.Wardrobe	Is greater than	*0*
Or	Order Details.Drawers	Is greater than	*0*
Or	Order Details.CoffeeTable	Is greater than	*0*
Or	Order Details.Kitchen	Is greater than	*0*
And	Customers.Town	Equals	Cullenstown

Each criterion you add through the *Add Criteria* dialog box is combined with all the other criteria you have already entered using the selected logical operator.
By adding the *AND Customers.Town Equals Cullenstown* criterion last, you combine this requirement with all of the *Order Details* criteria. You could not have done this if you had added the *Town* criterion first.
When you have finished adding criteria, click **Close**.

8) Select **File | Return Data to Microsoft Excel**, or click the **Return Data** toolbar button.

Return Data button

9) Save your workbook.

Well done! You just created an advanced filter in MS Query, combining a range of criteria using both logical AND and logical OR.

Microsoft Query allows you to select any column in the database when you create a criterion, not only those that you are importing. This makes Microsoft Query a more powerful filtering tool than the *Query Wizard*.

Over to you: mandatory

Next, you will edit the query results on the *OUTDOOR* worksheet to show similar results.

- On the *OUTDOOR* worksheet of MFPF_ORD.XLS, add an advanced filter to the query results to show records for customers in Cullenstown who ordered at least one item of outdoor furniture.

- Save your workbook.

Chapter summary

A delimited text file is a text file in which columns of information are separated from each other by a particular character or set of characters, known as delimiters. Excel allows you to import data from delimited text files using the *Text Import Wizard*. You can choose to import all of the columns in a delimited text file, or only a subset of them. You can also specify at which row of the text file you should start the import.

Excel also allows you to import database records using a *query*. A query is a set of rules that specifies what records, or parts of records, to retrieve from the database, and how to display those data.

When you create a query, you can define a *sort order* for the results. You can sort by the values in any number of columns.

You can also include a filter in your query to import only those records that satisfy specific criteria. Excel's *Query Wizard* allows you to set simple filter requirements based on the values in the database columns you are importing. You can edit your query in Microsoft Query to set much more complex filter requirements based on the values in any of the database columns.

4

Sorting Data in a Spreadsheet

In this chapter

In ECDL 3, you learned how to sort the information in a column numerically and alphabetically, in ascending and descending order.

When you defined a query in Chapter 3, you edited that query to sort the returned data by the values in multiple columns. Now you will find out how to sort by multiple columns in an Excel spreadsheet.

You will learn how to use Excel's custom sort orders to sort data in a non-alphabetic and non-numeric order – for example, by days of the week.

Finally, you will learn how to define a custom sort order of your own.

New skills

At the end of this chapter you should be able to:

- Sort by the values in multiple columns
- Sort columns using a custom sort order
- Create a custom list

New words

At the end of this chapter you should be able to explain the following term:

- Custom list

Sorting data in Excel

Typically, you will sort data in an Excel spreadsheet so that they are presented in a way that is easier to read and understand. For example, you might sort a list of birthdays in chronological order, or a list of mountain ranges by height.

In ECDL 3, you used Excel's **Sort** command to sort the data in a single column into ascending or descending order. In fact, you can sort data by the values in up to three columns in Excel.

> **Note:** When you sorted records in a database query, there was no limit to the number of columns you could sort by.

Sorting multiple columns at the same time

Mrs Murphy liked the way you sorted the results from the query you created earlier. She would like to see the data on the *COMPLETE* worksheet of MFPF_ORD.XLS sorted by customer, with the orders from each customer sorted in reverse chronological order.

In the following exercise, you will rearrange the rows on the *COMPLETE* worksheet of MFPF_ORD.XLS as Mrs Murphy asked.

Exercise 4.1: Sorting by multiple columns

1) Open MFPF_ORD.XLS and go to the COMPLETE worksheet.

2) Select columns *A* to *J*, then select **Data | Sort ...** .
   The *Sort* dialog box opens.

3) In the *Sort by* field, select *CompanyName* and *Ascending*.
   In the *Then by* field, select *OrderDate* and *Descending*.

4) Click **OK**.

Your data are now sorted alphabetically by the values in the *CompanyName* column, with the orders for each company listed in reverse chronological order.

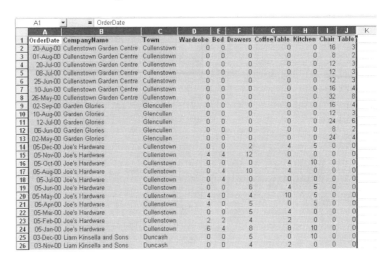

OrderDate	CompanyName	Town	Wardrobe	Bed	Drawers	CoffeeTable	Kitchen	Chair	Table
20-Aug-00	Cullenstown Garden Centre	Cullenstown	0	0	0	0	0	16	3
01-Aug-00	Cullenstown Garden Centre	Cullenstown	0	0	0	0	0	8	2
20-Jul-00	Cullenstown Garden Centre	Cullenstown	0	0	0	0	0	12	3
08-Jul-00	Cullenstown Garden Centre	Cullenstown	0	0	0	0	0	12	3
25-Jun-00	Cullenstown Garden Centre	Cullenstown	0	0	0	0	0	12	3
10-Jun-00	Cullenstown Garden Centre	Cullenstown	0	0	0	0	0	16	4
26-May-00	Cullenstown Garden Centre	Cullenstown	0	0	0	0	0	32	8
02-Sep-00	Garden Glories	Glencullen	0	0	0	0	0	16	4
10-Aug-00	Garden Glories	Glencullen	0	0	0	0	0	12	3
12-Jul-00	Garden Glories	Glencullen	0	0	0	0	0	24	6
06-Jun-00	Garden Glories	Glencullen	0	0	0	0	0	8	2
02-May-00	Garden Glories	Glencullen	0	0	0	0	0	24	4
05-Dec-00	Joe's Hardware	Cullenstown	0	0	2	4	5	0	0
05-Nov-00	Joe's Hardware	Cullenstown	4	4	12	0	0	0	0
05-Oct-00	Joe's Hardware	Cullenstown	0	0	0	4	10	0	0
05-Aug-00	Joe's Hardware	Cullenstown	0	4	10	4	0	0	0
05-Jul-00	Joe's Hardware	Cullenstown	0	4	0	0	0	0	0
05-Jun-00	Joe's Hardware	Cullenstown	0	0	6	4	5	0	0
05-May-00	Joe's Hardware	Cullenstown	4	0	4	10	5	0	0
05-Apr-00	Joe's Hardware	Cullenstown	4	0	5	0	5	0	0
05-Mar-00	Joe's Hardware	Cullenstown	0	0	5	4	0	0	0
05-Feb-00	Joe's Hardware	Cullenstown	2	2	4	2	0	0	0
05-Jan-00	Joe's Hardware	Cullenstown	6	4	8	8	10	0	0
03-Dec-00	Liam Kinsella and Sons	Duncash	0	0	5	0	10	0	0
03-Nov-00	Liam Kinsella and Sons	Duncash	0	0	4	2	0	0	0

5) Save your workbook when you are done.

Over to you: optional

To impress Mrs Murphy even more, you decide to rearrange the data on the *COMPLETE* worksheet again, this time sorting by three columns.

■ First, you will sort by *Town* in ascending order, then by *CompanyName* in ascending order, and finally by *OrderDate* in descending order.

All of the orders for each customer will still be grouped together, as Mrs Murphy requested, but now the customers themselves will be grouped according to which town they are from.

Custom sort orders

Look at the following column of data, which lists the first three months of the year in an arbitrary order:

	A	B	C
1	January		
2	March		
3	February		
4			

What order do you think it should be sorted in? If you tried simply to sort the months in ascending order, Excel would sort them alphabetically, resulting in:

	A	B	C
1	February		
2	January		
3	March		
4			

Chances are, you would rather sort the data so that they appeared in this order:

	A	B	C
1	January		
2	February		
3	March		
4			

How do you tell Excel that you want to use a special order for sorting columns containing the months of the year? You use a custom sort order.

Using a custom sort order

A custom sort order is defined using a custom list that lists the values in the required order. Excel comes with custom lists for days of the week and months of the year by default.

Custom list

A custom list is a list that specifies a non-alphabetic and non-numeric order for a series of data elements – for example, the days of the week in chronological order.

Custom lists are used when performing custom sorts and can also be used to autofill cell ranges. You learned about AutoFill functionality in ECDL 3.

In the next exercise, you will use a custom sort order to sort cells containing entries for the months January, February and March into their usual chronological order.

Exercise 4.2: Sorting using a custom sort order

1) Open a new workbook based on the default template.

2) In the cell range *A1:A3*, enter the values *January*, *March*, *February*.

3) Select the cell range, and select **Data | Sort ...** .
The *Sort* dialog box opens.

4) In the *Sort by* field, select *Column A*.

5) Click **Options ...** .
The *Sort Options* dialog box opens.

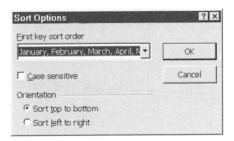

6) In the *First key sort order* field, select the entry beginning *January, February, March*, then click **OK**.

7) Click **OK**.
The data in the cell range are now sorted in the order you would usually expect.

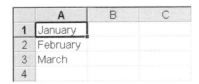

8) Close your workbook without saving when you are done.

Defining a custom list

You can add any number of additional custom lists to Excel; for example, you can list employee names by seniority, or groceries according to which aisle they are in in the supermarket. Custom lists are stored as part of Excel and will be available to you in any workbook.

Mr Murphy has heard about your superior sorting skills. He asks you to sort order information by how far away each customer is. This will let him stock the delivery van so that the goods for the cutomer furthest away are loaded first and unloaded last.

In the next exercise you will create a custom list that lists the customers in order of how far away they are.

Exercise 4.3: Adding a custom list to Excel

1) Start Excel if it is not already started. It does not matter which workbook is open, because your custom list will be stored as part of Excel.

2) Select **Tools | Options ...** .
   The *Options* dialog box opens.

3) Select the **Custom lists** tab.
   The custom lists already known to Excel are shown in the *Custom lists* area.

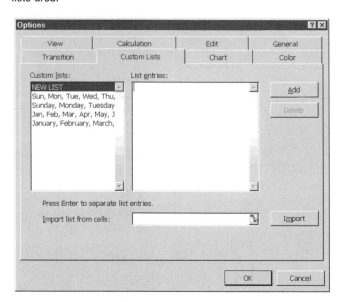

4) In the *Custom lists* area, select *NEW LIST*, then add the following data in the *List entries* area:
    Joe's Hardware
    Cullenstown Garden Centre
    The DIY Centre
    Mullens
    Garden Glories
    Liam Kinsella and Sons

    Pay close attention to the spelling and punctuation used. Later, Excel will use this list to sort entries in your spreadsheet, and it will not recognize values that do not exactly match those in this list.

5) Click **Add**.
    Your new entry is now shown in the *Custom lists* area.

6) Click **OK**.

Well done! You just added a custom list to Excel. You will be able to use this list in future to specify a custom sort order when you sort data or autofill cell ranges in any spreadsheet.

Over to you: optional

Next, you will sort the data on the *COMPLETE* worksheet by customer name, using the custom list you just defined to specify the correct sort order.

■   Use the custom list of customer names you defined in *Exercise 4.3* on page 34 to sort the entries on the *COMPLETE* worksheet in MFPF_ORD.XLS.

Chapter summary

Excel's sort facility allows you to reorder the rows in a spreadsheet according to the values in multiple columns. You can choose to sort data in ascending or descending alphabetic or numeric order, or in a custom order.

Custom sort orders allow you to sort data in a specific non-alphabetic and non-numeric order. Custom sorts use custom lists to define the correct order to use when sorting data.

A custom list is a list that specifies a non-alphabetic and non-numeric order for a series of data elements – for example, the days of the week in chronological order.

You can create your own custom lists in Excel.

5

Naming Cells and Adding Comments

When dealing with large spreadsheets, it is easy to lose track of what particular cell ranges are for, and why you have decided to perform your calculations in a particular way.

Usually, you use labels to indicate what the contents of a particular cell, row or column represent. Sometimes, because of the layout or complexity of your data, it might not be possible to label them in this way. For example, you may want to assign a single overall label to a group of labelled cells or cell ranges.

In this chapter you will learn about two other ways you can assign additional information to a cell or cell range: custom names and comments.

New skills

At the end of this chapter you should be able to:

- Give a cell or cell range a custom name
- Navigate a worksheet or workbook using custom names
- Use a named cell or cell range in a formula
- Add comments to your spreadsheet
- Read comments in a spreadsheet
- Edit spreadsheet comments
- Delete spreadsheet comments

New words

At the end of this chapter you should be able to explain the following terms:

- Custom name
- Comment

Cell names

Every cell in a worksheet has a unique name.

By default, a cell's name is determined by the column and row it occupies. For example, *A1* is the default name of the cell that appears in column *A* of row *1* in every Excel worksheet.

When you select a cell, its name appears in the *Name Box* to the left of the formula bar.

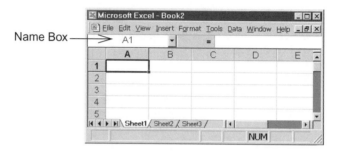

You can also enter a cell's name in the *Name Box* and press **Enter** to select that cell.

Custom cell names

You can associate a custom name with any cell or cell range. Because cell names must be unique, you can only use a particular name once in any workbook. But you can associate as many different custom names as you like with any cell or cell range.

> **Custom name**
>
> *A custom name is a unique name in a workbook that can be used to identify a cell or cell range.*

You can see a list of all of the custom names associated with cells and cell ranges in your workbook by clicking the down arrow to the right of the *Name Box*. If you select a name from this list, Excel will instantly select the cell or cell range that uses that name.

Custom cell names and formulae

You can use custom cell names instead of the default ones when you refer to cells and cell ranges in formulae. This can often make formulae easier to read and to edit.

Have a look at cell *C15*, which has been named *INC_TOT*, on the *INCOMING* worksheet of MFPF_FINANCE.XLS. It contains the formula:

=SUM(Products)+SUM(Delivery)

Compare this with:

=SUM(B2:B13)+SUM(C2:C13)

Although each formula calculates exactly the same thing, the first is much easier to understand.

Assigning a custom name to a cell range

There are a lot of data in the MFPF_FINANCE.XLS workbook. Naming particular cells and cell ranges will make the workbook easier to use.

In the next exercise, you are going to assign a custom name to a cell range.

Exercise 5.1: Naming a cell range

1) Open MFPF_FINANCE.XLS and go to the *SALES TOTALS* worksheet.

2) Select the cell range *A1:H13*.
   This cell range will be used to hold the monthly sales figures for each product.

3) In the *Name Box*, enter the word *SALES* and press **Enter**.

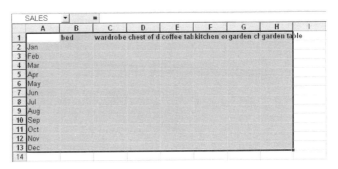

4) Save the workbook.

If you look at the *Name Box* list, *SALES* is now included.

The procedure for naming a single cell is exactly the same.

Next, you will name some cell ranges yourself, and then use the custom names in a formula.

- On the *OUTGOING* worksheet of MFPF_FINANCE.XLS, name the cell ranges referring to particular payment types (for example, assign the name *RENT* to the cell range *B2:B13*).

- Enter a formula in cell *C15* that adds up the totals for each payment type for the year, using the cell range names you just defined.

- Assign the name *TOTAL_OUTGOING* to cell *C15*; then save your workbook.

Comments

Comments are a useful way to add notes to cells in your worksheets. You might add a comment to remind yourself of why you calculated a value using one method rather than another. Or you might use a comment to let a colleague who will work with the spreadsheet later know what needs to be done next.

> **Comment**
>
> *A comment is a type of note that can be associated with a spreadsheet cell.*

Comment text is normally hidden from view, so that you can continue working with an uncluttered spreadsheet. A cell with an associated comment has a small red triangle in its top right corner:

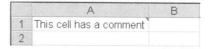

The *Reviewing* toolbar contains buttons for most of the commands you will use when creating, reading, editing and deleting comments. If you cannot see the *Reviewing* toolbar, you can open it by selecting **View | Toolbars | Reviewing**.

Adding comments

Earlier, you assigned the name *SALES* to a cell range in MFPF_FINANCE.XLS. At the moment, there are no numeric data in this cell range. What is the cell range there for? How will someone else editing the worksheet know if it will be required later, or if you have already used it and it can be deleted?

In the next exercise, you will add a comment to the *SALES* cell range explaining what it represents and what it will be used for.

Exercise 5.2: Adding a comment to a cell

1) Go to the cell range named *SALES* in MFPF_FINANCE.XLS.

2) Right-click cell *A1*, and select **Insert Comment** from the shortcut menu that appears.
   – or –
   Select cell *A1* and click the **New Comment** button on the *Reviewing* toolbar.
   A comment box opens.

New Comment button

3) Enter the following text in the comment box:
   This table shows the total sales of each product type each month. The data will be used later to calculate our incoming sales revenue on the INCOMING worksheet.

4) If you cannot see all of the comment text, resize the comment box by clicking and dragging one of the white resize handles that appear around the edge of the box.

5) Save your workbook when you are done.

Reading comments

There are several different ways to display the comment associated with a cell in order to read it:

- If you place your cursor over the cell with the comment, a pop-up box displays the contents of the comment. The pop-up box closes when you move your cursor away.

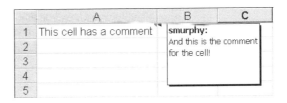

Show/Hide
Comment button

- If you select the cell with the comment, you can click the **Show/Hide Comment** button on the *Reviewing* toolbar to display the comment associated with that cell. The comment will remain open until you click the **Show/Hide Comment** button a second time.

- If you right-click a cell with an associated comment, you can select **Show Comment** from the shortcut menu that opens. The comment will remain open until you right-click the cell again and select **Hide Comment** from the shortcut menu.

You can also choose to display all spreadsheet comments. There are two ways to do this:

- If you select **View | Comments**, all comments will be displayed. You can deselect **View | Comments** to hide all comments again.

Show/Hide All
Comments button

- If you click the **Show/Hide All Comments** button on the *Reviewing* toolbar, all comments will be displayed. Click the **Show/Hide All Comments** button again to hide the comments.

Editing comments

You can reopen a comment to edit its text at any time.

In the next exercise, you will edit the comment you added to the *SALES* cell range in *Exercise 5.2* on page 41.

Exercise 5.3: Editing a comment

1) Go to the cell range named *SALES* in MFPF_FINANCE.XLS.

2) Right-click cell *A1*, and select **Edit Comment** from the shortcut menu that appears.
   – or –

Edit Comment button

Select cell *A1* and click the **Edit Comment** button on the *Reviewing* toolbar.
The comment box opens for editing.

3) Go to the end of the text you entered earlier and add the following text: *and also our materials expenses on the OUTGOING worksheet*.

4) Save your workbook when you are done.

Deleting comments

If you select a cell with an associated comment and press **Delete**, you delete the cell contents but not the comment. This means that you can add a comment saying what the value in the cell represents and not worry about losing your comment if you delete or change the value in the cell.

In the next exercise, you will find out how to delete the comment you added to the *SALES* cell range in *Exercise 5.2* on page 41.

Exercise 5.4: Removing a comment

1) Go to the cell range named *SALES* in MFPF_FINANCE.XLS.

2) Right-click cell *A1*, and select **Delete Comment** from the shortcut menu that appears.
    – or –

Delete Comment button

Select cell *A1* and click the **Delete Comment** button on the *Reviewing* toolbar.
The comment is deleted from the cell.

3) Save and close your workbook when you are done.

Chapter summary

Every cell in every Excel worksheet has a default name that is defined by the column and row it is in – for example, *A1*. You can assign a unique custom name to a cell or cell range. These custom names can be used in formulae.

A comment is a type of note that can be associated with a spreadsheet cell. A small red triangle in a cell indicates that it has an associated comment. Usually comments are hidden so that you can work with an uncluttered worksheet.

6

Using Paste Special

In this chapter

Every cell in an Excel spreadsheet has many different types of information associated with it. It will have some kind of formatting. It may contain a value or formula, or an associated comment.

Usually, when you copy a cell's contents and paste them somewhere else, you paste all of the information associated with that cell.

Excel's **Paste Special** command allows you to select specific elements of a copied cell's information to paste. You can also manipulate copied data in a variety of ways before pasting them to their destination cell.

New skills

At the end of this chapter you should be able to:

- Paste specific elements of copied data to a destination cell
- Perform simple mathematical operations using **Paste Special**
- Create links between cells using **Paste Special**

New words

There are no new words in this chapter.

Why Paste Special?

When you copy data from a cell in an Excel spreadsheet, and paste them to another cell, Excel pastes *all* of the data associated with the cell you copied to the new cell.

If you copied the value 12, formatted in 14-point Arial with a bright yellow background, then when you paste the value to a new cell, it will be formatted in 14-point Arial with a bright yellow background. If the value in the cell you copied was the result of a formula, you probably will not even get the same value when you paste it, unless the formula used absolute cell references.

When you use the **Paste Special** command instead of **Paste**, the *Paste Special* dialog box opens, and you can choose which part or parts of the data you really want to paste.

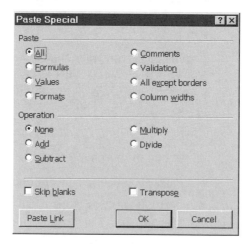

Note: If you are pasting data other than Excel spreadsheet cells, **Edit | Paste Special** opens the standard *Paste Special* dialog box common to all Microsoft Office software.

Pasting different types of information

In the *Paste* area of the *Paste Special* dialog box, you can choose which part, or parts, of the copied data you want to paste to the destination cells.

You can only choose one option at a time from the *Paste* area. If you want to paste a combination of the data elements – for example, a formula and its associated comment – you must use **Paste Special** more than once to paste each piece of data.

The following table lists the different options in the *Paste* area of the *Paste Special* dialog box and explains what each one does.

Option	Action
All	Paste all data from the copied cell.
Formulas	Paste the formula from the copied cell, if there is one. Paste the value from the copied cell if there is no formula.
Values	Paste the value from the copied cell. If the copied cell contains a formula, paste the result of that formula as a value.
Formats	Paste the formatting data from the copied cell.
Comments	Paste the comment from the copied cell.
Validation	Paste the validation, or data entry, rules from the copied cell.
All except borders	Paste the formula (or value if there is no formula) and the formatting data from the copied cell, but do not include border formatting.
Column widths	Paste the column width from the copied cell.

In the following exercises, you will copy cells from the workbook PASTE_SPECIAL.XLS, and use the options in the *Paste Special* dialog box to paste particular parts of the copied data to destination cells.

> **Note:** To deselect a cell range after you have copied it, press **Esc**.

Exercise 6.1: Pasting formulae

1) Open the PASTE_SPECIAL.XLS workbook.

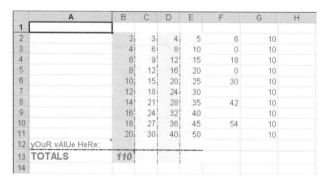

	A	B	C	D	E	F	G	H
1								
2		2	3	4	5	6	10	
3		4	6	8	10	0	10	
4		6	9	12	15	18	10	
5		8	12	16	20	0	10	
6		10	15	20	25	30	10	
7		12	18	24	30		10	
8		14	21	28	35	42	10	
9		16	24	32	40		10	
10		18	27	36	45	54	10	
11		20	30	40	50		10	
12	yOuR vAlUe HeRe:							
13	TOTALS	110						
14								

2) Copy the contents of cell *B13*.

3) Select the cell range *C13:E13*.

4) Select **Edit | Paste Special**.

5) In the *Paste* area, select *Formulas* and click **OK**.
   The relative SUM formula from cell *B13* is the only piece of data pasted to the cells in the cell range *C13:E13*.

Exercise 6.2: Pasting values

1) Copy the contents of cell *B13*.

2) Select cell *J2*.

3) Select **Edit | Paste Special**.

4) In the *Paste* area, select *Values* and click **OK**.
   The result of the formula in cell *B13* is pasted to cell *J2*.

Exercise 6.3: Pasting formats

1) Copy the contents of cell *A13*.

2) Select the cell range *C13:E13*.

3) Select **Edit | Paste Special**.

4) In the *Paste* area, select *Formats* and click **OK**.
   The cell and font formatting from cell *A13* is pasted to cells *C13:E13*.

Exercise 6.4: Pasting all cell information except borders

1) Copy the cell range named *Table1*.

2) Select cell *B15*.

3) Select **Edit | Paste Special**.

4) In the *Paste* area, select *All except borders* and click **OK**.
   All of the copied cell information except borders is pasted to a cell range starting in cell *B15*.

Exercise 6.5: Pasting column widths

1) Copy the cell range named *Table1*.

2) Select cell *H15*.

3) Select **Edit | Paste Special**.

4) In the *Paste* area, select *Column widths* and click **OK**.
   The column widths used in *Table1* are pasted to a cell range starting in cell *H15*.

Exercise 6.6: Pasting comments

1) Copy the contents of cell *A13*.

2) Select the cell range *C13:E13*.

3) Select **Edit | Paste Special**.

4) In the *Paste* area, select *Comments* and click **OK**.
   The comment in cell *B13* is pasted to cells *C13:E13*.

Exercise 6.7: Pasting validation

1) Copy the contents of cell *B12*.
   Cell *B12* has associated validation rules that allow you to enter only whole numbers in the cell.

2) Select the cell range *C12:E12*.

3) Select **Edit | Paste Special**.

4) In the *Paste* area, select *Validation* and click **OK**.
   The validation rules from cell *B12* are pasted to cells *C12:E12*.

The Operation area

You can combine numeric data from a copied cell with numeric data in a destination cell when you use **Paste Special**. The value in the destination cell is replaced by the result of the operation. Available operations are listed in the *Operation* area of the *Paste Special* dialog box.

The selection you make in the *Operation* area is combined with your selection from the *Paste* area.

The following table lists the different options in the *Operation* area of the *Paste Special* dialog box and explains what each one does:

Option	Action
None	Do not perform any operation.
Add	Add the data in the copied cell to the data in the destination cell, and place the result in the destination cell.
Subtract	Subtract the data in the copied cell from the data in the destination cell, and place the result in the destination cell.
Multiply	Multiply the data in the copied cell by the data in the destination cell, and place the result in the destination cell.
Divide	Divide the data in the destination cell by the data in the copied cell, and place the result in the destination cell.

In the next exercise, you will use the *Add* operation in the *Paste Special* dialog box to combine numeric data in two cell ranges.

Exercise 6.8: Pasting with operations

1) Copy the contents of cells *B2:B11*.

2) Select the cell range *G2:G11*.

3) Select **Edit | Paste Special**.

4) In the *Paste* area, select *All*.
   In the *Operations* area, select *Add*.

5) Click **OK**.
   The values in the cells in the copied range are added to the values in the corresponding cells in the destination cell range, and the totals replace the original values in the cell range *G2:G11*.

Special options

There are three additional special options in the *Paste Special* dialog box: *Skip blanks*, *Transpose* and **Paste Link**.

Skip blanks

A 'blank' cell is one that contains no values or formulae, though it may have any of the other information types associated with it, such as formatting, comments or validation rules.

The *Skip blanks* option can be used in conjunction with options from the *Paste* and *Operation* areas of the *Paste Special* dialog box. If *Skip blanks* is selected, then no data are pasted for any copied cell that does not contain either a value or a formula.

If you try to divide a number by zero in Excel, an error message, *#DIV/0!*, appears in the cell where the calculation was attempted. When you use operations, blank cells are treated as though they contain zeros. The *Skip blanks* option is especially useful when used in combination with the *Divide* operation.

In the next exercise, you will use the *Skip blanks* option on the *Paste Special* dialog box to tell Excel to ignore blank cells in a copied cell range when performing a *Divide* operation.

Exercise 6.9: Skip blanks

1) Copy the contents of cells *F2:F11*.

2) Select the cell range *G2:G11*.

3) Select **Edit | Paste Special**.

4) In the *Paste* area, select *Values*.
   In the *Operations* area, select *Divide*.
   Check the box beside *Skip blanks*.
   Click **OK**.

	A	B	C	D	E	F	G	H
1								
2		2	3	4	5	6	2	
3		4	6	8	10	0	#DIV/0!	
4		6	9	12	15	18	0.888839	
5		0	12	16	20	0	#DIV/0!	
6		10	15	20	25	30	0.666667	
7		12	18	24	30		22	
8		14	21	28	35	42	0.571429	
9		16	24	32	40		26	
10		18	27	36	45	54	0.518519	
11		20	30	40	50		30	
12	yOuR vAlUe HeRe:							
13	TOTALS	110						
14								

In the cell range *G2:G11*, *#DIV/0!* errors are shown in the cells where you actually divided by zero.
Where the cell in the copied cell range was blank, the value in the pasted range does not change.

Transpose

You can combine the *Transpose* option with selections from the *Paste* and *Operation* areas of the *Paste Special* dialog box. If you copy a range of cells that are in a column orientation, you can use the *Transpose* option to paste them in a row orientation, and vice versa.

In the next exercise, you will copy a cell range in a column orientation, and use the *Transpose* option to paste it to another cell range in a row orientation.

Exercise 6.10: Transpose

1) Copy the contents of cells *G2:G11*.

2) Select the cell *A1*.

3) Select **Edit | Paste Special**.

4) In the *Paste* area, select *Values*.
   Check the box beside *Transpose*.
   Click **OK**.

5) The data from the column of cells *G2:G11* are pasted to the row of cells *A1:A10*.

Paste Link

If it is important that a cell in your spreadsheet should always contain the value from another cell, you can create a link from the second cell to the first. If the value in the first cell changes, the value in the second cell automatically updates to reflect the change.

You can use the **Paste Link** option in the *Paste Special* dialog box to link the destination cell to the copied cell.

In the next exercise, you will create links from cells in a destination range to cells in a source range using the **Paste Link** option.

Exercise 6.11: Paste link

1) Copy the contents of cells *A13:E13*.

2) Select the cell *H13*.

3) Select **Edit | Paste Special**.

4) Click **Paste Link**.
   A link is created from each of the cells in the range *H13:L13* to their corresponding cells in the source range, *A13:E13*.
   The values in cells *H13:L13* will update automatically to reflect changes to the values in cells *A13:E13*.

Over to you: optional

Continue to experiment with different combinations of options in the *Paste Special* dialog box, until you are comfortable with it. Save and close PASTE_SPECIAL.XLS when you are done.

Chapter summary

A cell in an Excel spreadsheet has many different types of information associated with it: values, formatting, comments, etc. When you use **Copy** and **Paste** to copy the contents of one cell to another in a worksheet, all of the different information types are pasted. You can use **Paste Special** to select a subset of the information types to paste.

Paste Special allows you to combine numeric data from copied cells with numeric data in destination cells using simple mathematical operations. The results of the operation replace the original values in the destination cells.

The *Skip blanks* option allows you to choose not to paste any information from blank copied cells. A blank cell is one that contains no value or formula, though it may contain other information, such as formatting or a comment.

The *Transpose* option allows you to change the orientation of the copied cells when you paste them, from row to column or from column to row.

The **Paste Link** option allows you to create a link from a destination cell to a source cell. The value in the destination cell will update automatically if the value or formula in the source cell changes.

7

Summarizing Data Using PivotTables

In this chapter

Occasionally, you will want to create a report summarizing the data in a spreadsheet. Your report will probably perform a particular type of calculation using the data. You might even want to filter the data you include in a particular calculation.

Where the spreadsheets you are working with are large and detailed, creating a summary report can be a complicated and demanding task.

Excel's PivotTable functionality allows you to create dynamic, interactive summaries of a set of data.

In this chapter, you will learn how to create and use PivotTables.

New skills

At the end of this chapter you should be able to:

- Create a PivotTable
- Filter data in a PivotTable
- Group data in a PivotTable
- Refresh a PivotTable

New words

At the end of this chapter you should be able to explain the following terms:

- PivotTable
- Field
- Group

What are PivotTables?

A PivotTable is a useful Excel tool for summarizing large amounts of information in a dynamic report.

PivotTable
A PivotTable is an interactive table that allows you to dynamically create reports summarizing large amounts of data.

PivotTables can be used to generate reports on data from external databases or from Excel spreadsheets. You do not need to include all of the columns from your data source in a PivotTable, only the ones that are of interest to you.

The columns in your original data are referred to as fields when you include them in a PivotTable. This is to avoid confusion with the columns of the PivotTable itself.

Field
A field in a PivotTable corresponds to a column in the data source that the PivotTable is being used to summarize.

You can select the field or fields on which summary calculations should be performed. Summary functions include sum, average, minimum and maximum.

PivotTable layout

When you define the layout for a PivotTable, you add fields to four areas: *Page*, *Row*, *Column* and *Data*.

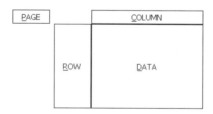

The *Page*, *Column* and *Row* areas show the fields you add and their different values. These values act as labels for the summary results, which are calculated in the *Data* area.

You can use the fields in the *Row*, *Column* and *Page* areas to filter the records from the data source that are included in the PivotTable.

Each field in the *Data* area must have a data function associated with it. This function determines what type of summary result is shown for that field. You can calculate more than one type of summary value from the data in any field.

You do not have to add fields to the *Page*, *Row* and *Column* areas, but the *Data* area must contain at least one field and an associated data function.

Filtering using fields

If you click the arrow to the right of any field name in a PivotTable, you open a drop-down list that contains a list of all the possible values that field might have. The list of values is determined by the values in the records in your data source.

You can check or uncheck the box beside each value to include or exclude records in which the field has that value.

When you have finished making your selections, click **OK** to return to the PivotTable, which will now only display records matching those values.

The drop-down list for a *Page* field is slightly different: it does not have checkboxes beside each value. You can only select one value at a time. But it does have an extra value, *All*, which allows you to include all possible values for the field.

Here is an example of a PivotTable that is based on the data in the *COMPLETE* worksheet of MFPF_ORD.XLS:

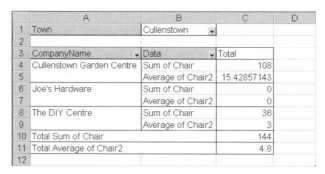

	A	B	C	D
1	Town	Cullenstown ▾		
2				
3	CompanyName ▾	Data ▾	Total	
4	Cullenstown Garden Centre	Sum of Chair	108	
5		Average of Chair2	15.42857143	
6	Joe's Hardware	Sum of Chair	0	
7		Average of Chair2	0	
8	The DIY Centre	Sum of Chair	36	
9		Average of Chair2	3	
10	Total Sum of Chair		144	
11	Total Average of Chair2		4.8	
12				

This PivotTable calculates:

- The total number of chairs ordered by each company over the year.

- The average number of chairs ordered by each company per order.

The *Town* field is used in the *Page* area, and the *CompanyName* field in the *Row* area. The *Town* field has been used to filter results in the table to show those from customers in *Cullenstown* only.

The *Data* area includes two different calculations on the data in the *Chair* field: one to calculate the sum, and one to calculate the average. When a field is used more than once in a single PivotTable, it is relabelled to include a number, for example, *Chair* and *Chair2* in the example shown.

At the bottom of the PivotTable, grand totals show the total number of chairs ordered, and the average number of chairs per order.

Creating PivotTables

You need to produce figures that show MFPF's total sales for each product by month to add to the *SALES TOTALS* worksheet of MFPF_FINANCE.XLS.

In the next exercise, you will begin to calculate these totals by creating a PivotTable to summarize the sales data in the cell range *A1:J55* on the *COMPLETE* worksheet of MFPF_ORD.XLS.

Exercise 7.1: Creating a PivotTable

1) Open MFPF_ORD.XLS.

2) Select **Data | PivotTable and PivotChart Report ...** .
   – or –

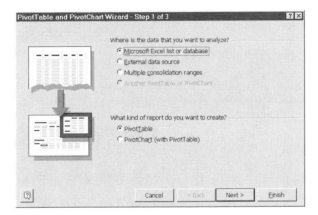

   Click the **PivotTable Wizard** button on the *PivotTable* toolbar.
   If you cannot see the *PivotTable* toolbar, you can open it by selecting
   View | Toolbars | PivotTable.
   The *PivotTable and PivotChart Wizard* opens.

PivotTable
Wizard button

3) In the *Where is the data that you want to analyze?* area, select
   Microsoft Excel list or database.
   In the *What kind of report do you want to create?* area, select
   PivotTable.
   Click **Next**.
   A dialog box opens where you can specify the cell range that contains
   the source data for the PivotTable.

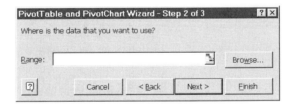

4) Open the *COMPLETE* worksheet and select the cell range *A1:J55*. The
   reference for the cell range is automatically filled in to the *Range* field.
   Click **Next**.

A dialog box opens where you can select where to put your PivotTable.

5) Specify that you want to put the PivotTable on a *New worksheet*.

6) Click **Layout**.
The *PivotTable and PivotChart Wizard – Layout* dialog box opens.

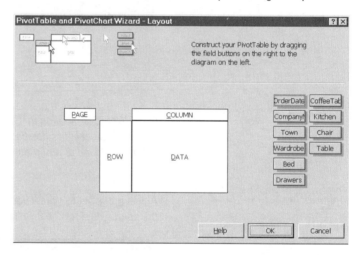

7) You add fields to different areas of the PivotTable by dragging the buttons from the right-hand side of the dialog box to the PivotTable diagram on the left.

- Drag **OrderDate** to the *Row* area.

- Drag the following (in order) to the *Data* area: **Bed, Wardrobe, Drawers, CoffeeTable, Kitchen, Chair, Table.**
The fields in the *Data* area are labelled to indicate the data function associated with them.

For this exercise, they should all use the data function *Sum of*. You can change the data function for a field by double-clicking the field and selecting a function from the list that appears.
Click **OK**.

8) Click **Finish**.

The PivotTable is added to your workbook on a new worksheet. It is laid out according to the settings you made.

	A	B	C	D
1	Drop Page Fields Here			
2				
3	OrderDa ▼	Data ▼	Total	
4	03-Jan-00	Sum of Bed	6	
5		Sum of Wardrobe	0	
6		Sum of Drawers	12	
7		Sum of CoffeeTable	2	
8		Sum of Kitchen	0	
9		Sum of Chair	0	
10		Sum of Table	0	
11	05-Jan-00	Sum of Bed	4	
12		Sum of Wardrobe	6	
13		Sum of Drawers	8	
14		Sum of CoffeeTable	8	
15		Sum of Kitchen	10	
16		Sum of Chair	0	
17		Sum of Table	0	
18	24-Jan-00	Sum of Bed	0	
19		Sum of Wardrobe	0	
20		Sum of Drawers	8	
21		Sum of CoffeeTable	6	
22		Sum of Kitchen	10	
23		Sum of Chair	0	
24		Sum of Table	0	
25	03-Feb-00	Sum of Bed	0	
26		Sum of Wardrobe	2	
27		Sum of Drawers	2	

9) Name the new worksheet *PIVOT* and save your workbook.

Grouping data in PivotTables

You now have 360 rows of data showing sales totals for each furniture type on particular dates. You also have a grand total for sales of each furniture type for the year. You want to know the total for each month.

You could select a subset of *OrderDates* for each month and take the grand totals calculated for those, but that would take a lot of time and clicking.

Not to worry! Another feature of PivotTables is that you can group fields to make it easier to view or select subsets of information in one go.

Group
A group is a set of objects that is treated as a single object.

In the next exercise, you will create a group for all of the order dates in January.

Exercise 7.2: Grouping data in a PivotTable

1) In the *OrderDate* field, select the cells that contain a January date.

2) Right-click and select **Group and Outline | Group** from the shortcut menu that appears.
An extra field (*OrderDate2*) is added to the *Column* area of the PivotTable.
An entry in this column called *Group1* covers all the cells in *OrderDate* related to January.

	A	B	C	D	E
1					
2					
3	OrderDate2 ▾	OrderDate ▾	Data ▾	Total	
4	Group1	03-Jan-00	Sum of Bed	6	
5			Sum of Wardrobe	0	
6			Sum of Drawers	12	
7			Sum of CoffeeTable	2	
8			Sum of Kitchen	0	
9			Sum of Chair	0	
10			Sum of Table	0	
11		05-Jan-00	Sum of Bed	4	
12			Sum of Wardrobe	6	
13			Sum of Drawers	8	
14			Sum of CoffeeTable	8	
15			Sum of Kitchen	10	
16			Sum of Chair	0	
17			Sum of Table	0	
18		24-Jan-00	Sum of Bed	0	
19			Sum of Wardrobe	0	
20			Sum of Drawers	8	
21			Sum of CoffeeTable	6	
22			Sum of Kitchen	10	
23			Sum of Chair	0	
24			Sum of Table	0	
25	03/02/2000	03-Feb-00	Sum of Bed	0	
26			Sum of Wardrobe	2	

You can ungroup the dates in any group again by selecting the group, right-clicking, and selecting **Group and Outline | Ungroup** from the shortcut menu that appears.

3) Double-click the group name to hide the details of the group members in the *OrderDate* field.

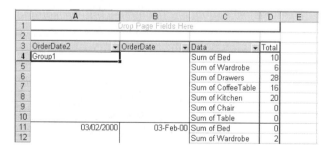

	A	B	C	D	E
1		Drop Page Fields Here			
2					
3	OrderDate2 ▾	OrderDate ▾	Data ▾	Total	
4	Group1		Sum of Bed	10	
5			Sum of Wardrobe	6	
6			Sum of Drawers	28	
7			Sum of CoffeeTable	16	
8			Sum of Kitchen	20	
9			Sum of Chair	0	
10			Sum of Table	0	
11	03/02/2000	03-Feb-00	Sum of Bed	0	
12			Sum of Wardrobe	2	

Now the numbers shown in the *Data* area refer to the month as a whole.

4) Select the text *Group1*, and in the formula bar enter the text *January* and press **ENTER**.
The group is renamed.

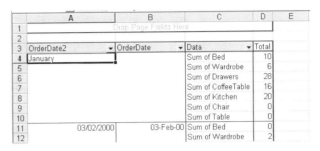

	A	B	C	D	E
1	Drop Page Fields Here				
2					
3	OrderDate2 ▼	OrderDate ▼	Data ▼	Total	
4	January		Sum of Bed	10	
5			Sum of Wardrobe	6	
6			Sum of Drawers	28	
7			Sum of CoffeeTable	16	
8			Sum of Kitchen	20	
9			Sum of Chair	0	
10			Sum of Table	0	
11	03/02/2000	03-Feb-00	Sum of Bed	0	
12			Sum of Wardrobe	2	

5) Save your workbook.

Over to you: mandatory

The PivotTable now displays sales totals for each furniture type for January and for all other dates in the year.

Next, you will finish grouping the PivotTable data and add the results you calculate to MFPF_FINANCE.XLS.

■ Group the dates for each of the other months together, hide the details in the *OrderDate* field, and rename the groups.

■ Finally, copy the monthly totals into the space left for them on the *SALES TOTALS* worksheet in the MFPF_FINANCE.XLS workbook. You will need to use **Edit | Paste Special** to paste the values and transpose them.

Save both workbooks when you are done.

Refresh PivotTables

In Chapter 3, you learned that you could update data imported from a delimited text file or from a database to match the source data at any time.

You can also refresh PivotTables so that they reflect the most current data in the data source defined.

In the next exercise, you will make a change to the sales data on the *COMPLETE* worksheet of MFPF_ORD.XLS and refresh your PivotTable to see this.

Don't worry – if you manually change the information in the PivotTable, you won't affect the database the results came from. In fact, you can refresh your PivotTable, and the values will change back to their original values again.

Exercise 7.3: Updating the data in a PivotTable

1) Go to the *COMPLETE* worksheet of MFPF_ORD.XLS.
   Change any one of the orders to include a request for 2000 wardrobes.

2) Go to the *PIVOT* worksheet.

3) Select **Data | Refresh Data**.

4) Look for the total that has been affected by the change you made.
   A month with in excess of 2000 wardrobe orders is easy to find!

Over to you: optional

Experiment with creating PivotTables to summarize the data on the *COMPLETE* worksheet of MFPF_ORD.XLS.

Here are some ideas for reports you could generate:

- A report showing the average order by a given customer for each furniture type in a year.
- A report showing the largest orders for specific furniture types by each company.
- A report showing the total sales of each furniture type in specific towns.

Chapter summary

A PivotTable is an interactive table that allows you to dynamically create reports summarizing large amounts of data.

PivotTables can be based on data from databases or from Excel spreadsheets.

A field in a PivotTable corresponds to a column in the data source that the PivotTable is based on.

You can group fields in a PivotTable to make it easier to view or select subsets of records. A group is a set of objects that is treated as a single object.

PivotTables can be refreshed at any time to reflect changes in their data source.

Linking Data in Spreadsheets

8

In this chapter

In Chapter 6, you created a link from one cell to the value in another using **Paste Special**. In this chapter you will find out how to create links between cells using link formulae.

You will also see how Excel charts remain linked to their source data, and how changes in the source values are reflected automatically in the charts.

Finally, you will learn how to add a link from a Word document to a cell range in an Excel spreadsheet.

New skills

At the end of this chapter you should be able to:

- Create links to cells on the same worksheet
- Create links to cells on other worksheets
- Create links to cells in other workbooks
- Add a chart linked to a cell range in one worksheet to any worksheet or workbook
- Create links from Word to cells in an Excel spreadsheet

New words

There are no new words in this chapter.

Linking to a cell on the same worksheet

You have used formulae in Excel before to perform calculations.

For example, the formula *=SUM(A1:A12)* uses the SUM function to add together the values in each cell in the range *A1:A12*, and displays the result.

When you create a link from one cell to another in an Excel spreadsheet, you use a link formula to refer to a cell's contents.

To create a link from one cell on a worksheet to another, you use a link formula in the form *=cellname*, for example, *=A1*.

If you had named the cell, you could refer to it by this custom name instead. The result would be the same; the data shown in the cell containing the link is the value in the linked cell.

In the next exercise, you will link a cell on the *OUTGOING* worksheet of MFPF_FINANCE.XLS to another cell on the same worksheet.

Exercise 8.1: Linking cells on a worksheet

1)   Open MFPF_FINANCE.XLS and go to the *OUTGOING* worksheet.

2)   In cell *A17*, enter the label *Outgoing total*.

3)   In cell *C17*, enter the link formula *=C15*.
     Cell *C17* is now linked to the value in cell *C15*.

4)   Enter number values in blank cells in the *Petrol* column and observe that the numbers in cells *C15* and *C17* both change.

Linking to cells in other worksheets

To create a link from a cell in one worksheet to a cell in another worksheet, you use the same principle, but you add an extra piece of information to your link formula that tells Excel which worksheet in the current workbook to look at.

A link from a cell in one worksheet to a cell in another worksheet in the same workbook is in the form *=sheetname!cellname* – for example, *=Sheet1!A1*.

A cell can have a default name and any number of custom names at the same time. A worksheet can only have one name, and this must be the name used in the link formula.

In the next exercise, you will create a link on the *PROFIT* worksheet of MFPF_FINANCE.XLS to the cell containing the value for total annual outgoings on the *OUTGOING* worksheet.

Exercise 8.2: Linking cells across worksheets

1) Go to the *PROFIT* worksheet of MFPF_FINANCE.XLS.

2) In cell *A17*, enter the label *Outgoing Total*.

3) In cell *C17*, enter the link formula *=OUTGOING!C17*.
   Cell *C17* is now linked to cell *C17* of the *OUTGOING* worksheet in the same workbook.

4) Delete the entries you added in the *Petrol* column on the *OUTGOING* worksheet in *Exercise 8.1* on page 66.
   The contents of cells *C15* and *C17* on the *OUTGOING* worksheet, and those of cell *C17* on the *PROFIT* sheet, update automatically to reflect your changes.

Linking to cells in other workbooks

You can even create a link from a cell in one workbook to a cell in another workbook. The link formula is in the form *=[bookname]sheetname!cellname* – for example, *=[book1.xls]sheet1!A1*.

> **Note:** If both workbooks are in the same folder, you only need to give the filename in the square brackets. If the files are in different folders, you will need to enter the full path, including filename, between the square brackets in the link formula.

Exercise 8.3: Linking cells across workbooks

1) Add a new worksheet to MFPF_FINANCE.XLS.

2) In cell *A1* on the new worksheet, enter the link
   =[MFPF_ORD.XLS]OUTDOOR!$A$1
   The value in cell *A1* on the *OUTDOOR* worksheet of MFPF_ORD.XLS now appears in cell *A1* of the new worksheet.

3) Delete the added worksheet, and save your workbook.

Cell references in formulae

The format used in link formulae to refer to cells in other worksheets and workbooks can be used in other formulae too.

For example, the following formula adds the contents of cell *A1* on *sheet1* of the current workbook to the contents of cell *A1* on *sheet1* of a workbook called *book1.xls*:
=sheet1!A1+[book1.xls]sheet1!A1.

Linking to cells in Excel workbooks from Word

Using Word's **Paste Special** command, you can create a link from a Word document to a cell range in an Excel workbook.

When you change the Excel spreadsheet, the linked data in the Word document are updated automatically to reflect your changes.

Mr Murphy is applying for a business loan to buy new machinery for the warehouse. He has already been to see the local bank manager, who has asked to see a summary of the business's incomings and outgoings for the previous year before agreeing to the loan. You have been asked to add these details to a letter Mr Murphy has written.

Although you have not finished working out the figures in MFPF_FINANCE.XLS, you do know which cell range they will go in.

You can add a link to the relevant cell range now, and then when you're finished making your calculations, all you will need to do is open the letter and print it. The data from the cell range in the workbook will be filled into the letter automatically.

In the next exercise, you will add a link from a letter written in a Word document to a cell range in the *PROFIT* worksheet of MFPF_FINANCE.XLS.

Exercise 8.4: Linking from Word to cells in a spreadsheet

1) Go to the *PROFIT* worksheet of MFPF_FINANCE.XLS.

2) Copy the cell range *A1:D15*.

3) Open the Word document LETTER.DOC, and go to the empty paragraph after the line 'I trust they will be to your satisfaction.'

4) Select **Edit | Paste Special** in Word.
The *Paste Special* dialog box opens.

5) Select *Paste link*, then select *Microscoft Excel Worksheet Object* from the *As* area.

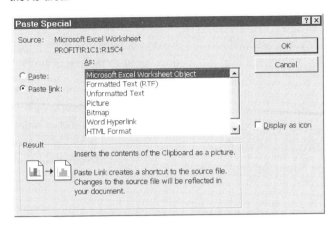

Click **OK**.
A link is added from the Word document to the copied cells in the Excel spreadsheet.
Your letter should now look like this:

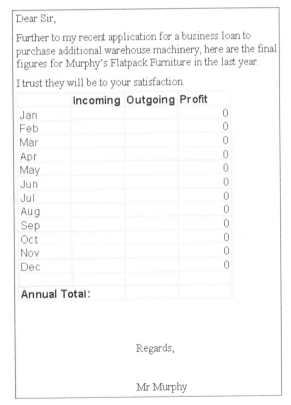

6) Save and close LETTER.DOC when you are done.

Note: You can create a link from a Word document to an Excel chart in exactly the same way.

Over to you: optional

Next, you will check that the link you created from the Word document to the Excel worksheet cell range really works.

■ Add some numbers to the *INCOMING* and *OUTGOING* columns in the *PROFIT* worksheet in MFPF_FINANCE.XLS. Open LETTER.DOC and check that the cells in the Word document have been updated to reflect your changes. Delete the numbers you added to the *PROFIT* worksheet when you are done.

Linking charts

When you create a chart in Excel, it is linked automatically to the source data from which it was generated. When you edit the source data, the chart updates automatically to reflect your changes.

When you create a chart, you are given the option of adding it to the current worksheet or to a new worksheet in the same workbook. To add the chart to another existing worksheet of the current workbook, or to a worksheet in a different workbook, you must use **Copy** and **Paste**. Copies of the chart remain linked to the source data.

In the following exercise, you will create a chart that shows MFPF's monthly telephone bill expenditure.

Exercise 8.5: Creating a linked chart

1) Go to the *OUTGOING* worksheet of MFPF_FINANCE.XLS.

2) Select the non-adjacent cell ranges *A2:A13* and *D2:D13*.
(To select non-adjacent cell ranges, select the first range, then holding down the **CTRL** key, select the second range.)

3) Select **Insert | Chart ...** .
– or –
Click the **Chart Wizard** button on the *Standard* toolbar.
The *Chart Wizard* opens.

Chart Wizard button

4) In the *Chart Wizard*, select *Column* in the *Chart type* field and click **Finish**.

5) A column chart indicating how much was spent on the telephone bill each month is inserted into the current worksheet.

In the next exercise, you will add copies of the chart you just created to a new worksheet in MFPF_FINANCE.XLS and to a worksheet in a new workbook. You will then edit the value of the phone bill for one month and see all three charts update to reflect that change.

Exercise 8.6: Creating copies of a linked chart

1) Select the chart you created in the last exercise.

2) Select **Edit | Copy**.

3) Select **Insert | Worksheet** to add a new worksheet to MFPF_FINANCE.XLS.

4) Open the new worksheet and select **Edit | Paste**.

5) Select **File | New ...** and create a new workbook based on the default template.

6) In the new workbook, paste the copied chart to the *Sheet1* worksheet in the new workbook.

7) Change the entry in cell *D3* on the *OUTGOING* worksheet in MFPF_FINANCE.XLS to – 10 and press **Enter**.
All three copies of the chart you created update to reflect the change.

When you are done, delete the entry in cell *D3* on the *OUTGOING* worksheet in MFPF_FINANCE.XLS.

Close all your workbooks without saving again when you are done.

Chapter summary

You can create a link from a cell in an Excel spreadsheet to any other cell in any worksheet in any workbook. The complete format for such links is *=[bookname]sheetname!cellname* – for example, *=[Book1.xls]Sheet1!A1*.

Charts created in Excel are linked automatically to the source data they were generated from. Even if a chart is copied to another worksheet or workbook, it remains linked to its source data and updates automatically to reflect changes in those data.

You can use Word's **Paste Special** command to create a link from a Word document to a cell range or chart in an Excel workbook. If the values in the cell range change, the values in the Word document update to reflect the changes.

Formatting your Spreadsheets

9

In this chapter

When you have added data to your spreadsheet, you will usually add some formatting to make the information clearer and more appealing to the eye.

In ECDL 3 you learned how to apply text and number formats to cells in an Excel spreadsheet.

In this chapter you will learn about other more advanced formatting options in Excel.

New skills

At the end of this chapter you should be able to:

- Freeze row and column titles
- Use Excel's AutoFormat option
- Create and apply a custom number format
- Use conditional formatting

New words

There are no new words in this chapter.

Freezing row and column titles

Where a spreadsheet contains many rows and columns, you may find that when you scroll down or across the worksheet, you are looking at a part of the spreadsheet where no row or column titles are visible. Unless the information in each column is very distinctive, for example, Name, Address and Telephone Number, the data may be difficult to read.

As an example, open MFPF_ORD.XLS, go to the *COMPLETE* worksheet, and look at cell *H50*. What does this number refer to? All the cells around it contain similar data. Unless you have a very large, high-resolution monitor, you probably cannot see the column title for the cell.

To determine what the number in the cell you are looking at refers to, you could scroll to the top of the sheet to see the column label and then scroll back again. But it would be good to be able to see the column labels all the time, no matter how far down the spreadsheet you scrolled.

Well, you can. Excel allows you to select a row, or set of rows, at the top of a spreadsheet and 'freeze' them so that you can see them no matter how far down the rest of the sheet you scroll. You can also freeze a column or group of columns at the left of the spreadsheet to have permanently visible row labels.

In the next exercise, you will create frozen column and row titles on the *COMPLETE* worksheet of MFPF_ORD.XLS.

Exercise 9.1: Freezing row and column titles

1) Open MFPF_ORD.XLS and go to the *COMPLETE* worksheet.

Vertical split box→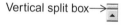

2) Click and drag the vertical split box, located at the top of the vertical scroll bar, to just below row 1.
The column titles are separated from the rest of the spreadsheet.

Horizontal split box

3) Click and drag the horizontal split box, located at the right of the horizontal scroll bar, to the right of column *B*.
The cells containing the *OrderDate* and *CompanyName* for each row are separated from the rest of the spreadsheet.

Your worksheet should now look like this:

With the worksheet divided in this way, you can scroll independently in each quadrant.

4)   Select **Window | Freeze panes**.
     The split dividers disappear and are replaced by lines.
     You can now only scroll in the lower right quadrant.

5)   Scroll down the worksheet. The frozen column titles remain visible no matter which rows you are looking at.
     Next, scroll across the worksheet. The frozen cells indicating the *OrderDate* and *CompanyName* for each order remain visible no matter which columns you are looking at.

6)   Save and close your workbook when you are done.

You can unfreeze areas by selecting **Window | Unfreeze Panes**. Then, to get rid of the split entirely, select **Window | Remove Split**.

Note: If you want to freeze horizontal and vertical portions of the screen, you must add both splits before freezing. Once a window has been frozen, you cannot split it again. You can only make one split in each direction.

Using AutoFormat

When you apply formatting to a spreadsheet, you can spend a lot of time deciding how you want your data to look, and then applying different fill colours, fonts, etc.

Excel's **AutoFormat** facility allows you to select one of 17 predefined design schemes and apply it to a cell range. Each scheme defines formats for numbers, borders, fonts, patterns, alignment, and cell width and height.

In the next exercise, you will format the accounting information on the *OUTGOING* worksheet of MFPF_FINANCE.XLS using an Excel **AutoFormat** option.

Exercise 9.2: Applying AutoFormat

1) Open MFPF_FINANCE.XLS and go to the *OUTGOING* worksheet.

2) Select the cell range *A1:G15*.

3) Select **Format | AutoFormat ...** .
   The *AutoFormat* dialog box opens.
   A sample of each format you can apply is shown in the left-hand panel of the dialog box, with its name below it.

4) Select the style *Classic 3* by clicking it once.
   A black border appears around the format to indicate that it has been selected.

5) Click **Options ...** .
   The *Formats to apply* area opens at the bottom of the dialog box, where you can specify a subset of the format elements of the format you want to use.

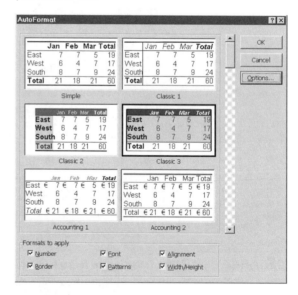

Deselect the *Border* option.
Each format preview changes to show how the format looks without borders.

6) Click **OK**.
   The *Classic 3* format is applied to the cell range *A1:G15* on the *OUTGOING* worksheet.

7) Save your workbook when you are done.

Over to you: optional

Try applying other **AutoFormat** styles to the cell range you just formatted. When you find one you like, apply the same format to the accounting information on the *INCOMING* and *PROFIT* worksheets.

Custom number formats

In ECDL 3 you learned how to apply number formats to cells in a worksheet to define how numeric data should appear – for example, with a certain number of decimal places, with a particular thousands indicator, or with a particular currency symbol.

If you want to use a number format that doesn't already exist in Excel, you can define a custom number format.

Mr Murphy has asked you to format numbers in a cell range in DELIVERIES.XLS as distances in kilometres. There is no default number style in Excel that will let you do this. If you just added the letters *km* to the numbers in each cell, the cell contents would be treated as text, and you would not be able to use the data in calculations later.

In the next exercise, you will create a custom number format to indicate kilometre distances, and then apply it to a cell range.

Exercise 9.3: Creating a custom number format

1) Open DELIVERIES.XLS and go to the *CHARGES* worksheet.

2) Select column *B*, which lists the distances to each customer's premises.

3) Select **Format | Cells** ... .
   – or –
   Click the **Format Cells** button on the *Formatting* toolbar.
   The *Format Cells* dialog box opens.

Format Cells button

4) Click the **Number** tab.

5) Select *Custom* in the *Category* list.

6) In the *Type* field, enter the text *0.0 "km"* (including the quotation marks) and press **Enter**.
   All the cells in column *B* that contain numeric data are now formatted to have one decimal place, and the letters *km* appear after the numbers.

7) Save and close your workbook when you are done.

Conditional formatting

Sometimes you will want to apply a certain type of formatting to data only if they satisfy certain criteria. For example, you might want to format every negative number in a cell range in bold, red text.

You could look at the values in each cell, identify the negative ones, and manually apply the required formatting to each one. Alternatively, you could use conditional formatting to automatically check the values in each cell of a cell range and format the negative ones in bold, red text.

You can also format the contents of one cell in a particular way if the value in another cell satisfies certain criteria.

For example, in cell *D9* on the *PERSONAL NOTES* worksheet of INVOICE_MFPF.XLT, the text *Late* has been entered and formatted in white so that it cannot be seen. The cell has conditional formatting associated with it: if the payment date in cell *C9* is more than 28 days after the invoice date in cell *C8*, then the text in this cell is formatted in red.

MFPF have estimated maximum payments for each utility. The estimated maximum for any electricity bill is £40. You have been asked to automatically flag any bill that exceeds that amount.

In the next exercise, you will apply conditional formatting to data in the *Electricity* column on the *OUTGOING* worksheet of MFPF_FINANCE.XLS, so that any payment exceeding £40 is shown in bold, red text.

Exercise 9.4: Applying conditional formatting

1) Go to the *OUTGOING* worksheet of MFPF_FINANCE.XLS.

2) Select the cell range *C2:C13*, which contains the values for electricity payments made by the business.

3) Select **Format | Conditional Formatting ...** .
    The *Conditional Formatting* dialog box opens.

4) In the *Condition 1* area of the *Conditional Formatting* dialog box, set the following condition:
Cell Value Is less than or equal to –40.
Remember, because the numbers on this worksheet indicate money that is being paid out by the business, they have been entered as negative values.

5) Click **Format ...** to open the *Format Cells* dialog box, where you will specify the format to apply if the condition is met.

6) In the *Format Cells* dialog box, select *Bold* in the *Font Style* area, and *Red* in the *Color* drop-down list.
Click **OK**.
You could add more conditional formatting rules to the cell by clicking **Add**. For now, you will only apply one conditional format.

7) Click **OK**.

8) Save your workbook.

The value in cell *C3* is now formatted in bold, red text as it exceeds the estimated maximum, as defined in *Condition 1*.

Over to you: optional

To impress the Murphys, you decide also to flag entries where the payment amount is close to the estimated maximum.

■ Apply conditional formatting rules to format payments of £39 and over in bold, orange text, and those of £38 and over in bold, yellow text.

Note: Excel applies formatting to the contents of a cell according to which of the defined conditions is satisfied first. Thus, the order in which you define your conditional formatting rules is important. £41 is obviously greater than £38, £39 and £40. If you specify the rules in the order given, £41 will be formatted in red; however, if you were to specify them in the reverse order, it would be formatted in yellow.

Chapter summary

Excel allows you to select a row, or set of rows, at the top of a spreadsheet and 'freeze' them so that you can see them no matter how far down the rest of the sheet you scroll. You can also freeze a column or group of columns at the left of the spreadsheet to have permanently visible row labels.

Excel's **AutoFormat** facility allows you to select one of 17 pre-defined design schemes and apply it to a cell range. Each scheme defines formats for numbers, borders, fonts, patterns, alignment, and cell width and height.

You can define custom number formats to use when formatting cells in Excel.

You can also use conditional formatting rules to format data in a certain way if they satisfy specified criteria.

10

Using Excel Macros

What are macros?

From time to time, you will want to perform the same series of actions on a cell or cell range in several worksheets.

For example, say you use Excel to keep track of all the phone calls you make in a month. Each month you create a new worksheet and add the numbers you dial in column *A* and the call durations in column *B*. At the end of the month, you sort the entries on the sheet by the number dialled, then apply different formatting to columns *A* and *B*. You also apply conditional formatting to column *B* to highlight any calls that went on for over an hour.

Because you perform these exact actions in exactly the same way every month, it would save you time in the long run to have a single Excel command that could perform this task.

Well, you can create a command that performs all of these actions and save it in Excel.

Excel allows you to record a series of actions that are always performed in the same way, and in the same order, and save the series as a new command, called a macro.

Macro
A macro is a custom command defined to perform a series of specific actions in the same way and in the same order every time the macro is run.

Macros are associated with Excel workbooks. You can save a macro in one of three places:

- Personal Macro Workbook – The Personal Macro Workbook is stored in the Excel start-up folder. Any macros you save in this workbook will be available to you whenever you run Excel, no matter what workbook you are editing.

- New Workbook – You can choose to create a new workbook and save the macro there. The macro will be available to you when you edit the new workbook.

- This Workbook – If you save the macro in the workbook you create it in, it will be available to you whenever you edit that workbook.

Note: If a workbook you open contains macros, a dialog box will appear alerting you to this fact, and asking if you want to enable or disable the macros. If you disable the macros, they cannot run. This allows you to protect yourself from macro viruses.

Recording macros

To record a macro in Excel, you first tell Excel to start recording what you are doing, then you perform the actions you want the macro to perform whenever you run it. When you have finished, you tell Excel to stop recording your actions. Everything you do from the time you tell Excel to start recording to when you tell it to stop is included in the macro.

If you apply formatting to a cell, then change your mind and change it to something else, both of the formatting actions are remembered and performed, in order, by the macro when it is run. Every action included in the macro increases its size, so you must be clear before you start recording exactly what it is that you want to record.

Another important aspect of macros is that they can be absolute or relative.

Absolute macros

An absolute macro is one that performs exactly the same set of actions on the exact same cell or cell range whenever it is run. An absolute macro might always change the format for columns *A* and *D*, or always delete the contents of the cell range *A3:D5*, for example.

Relative macros

A relative macro performs the set of recorded actions relative to the cell or cell range selected when you run the macro. A relative macro might assign a particular background colour, text colour, font and number format to the contents of the selected cell or cell range when it is run, for example.

Mr Murphy urgently needs the *COMPLETE*, *INDOOR* and *OUTDOOR* worksheets of MFPF_ORD.XLS reformatted. He has asked you to apply a certain type of formatting to all three sheets in the next five minutes.

You know that you can apply the required formatting to one of the sheets in five minutes, but you doubt you'll have time to format the other two sheets as well. But, if you record the changes you make to the first sheet in a macro, then you can reapply all of the changes to each of the other sheets in seconds.

In the next exercise, you will record an absolute macro to apply formatting to data imported using the MFPF_Q1.DQY query you created and saved earlier.

Exercise 10.1: Recording a macro

1) Open MFPF_ORD.XLS and go to the *COMPLETE* worksheet.

2) You will include commands to split and freeze the first row and first two columns of the selected worksheet in your formatting macro. To remove the freezes already applied to the data in the *COMPLETE* worksheet, select **Window | Unfreeze panes**, then select **Window | Remove Split**.
    Now you are ready to start recording your macro.

3) Select **Tools | Macros | Record New Macro ...** .
    The *Record Macro* dialog box opens.

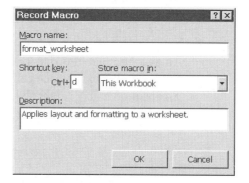

4) In the *Macro name* field, enter *format_worksheet*.
    In the *Shortcut key* field enter *d*.
    In the *Store macro in* field, select *This Workbook*.
    In the *Description* field, enter the text *Applies layout and formatting to a worksheet*.
    Click **OK**.
    The *Record Macro* dialog box closes, and the *Stop Recording* toolbar appears.

Everything you do from now until you stop recording will be saved in the new macro.

Relative Reference button

5) You want to record an absolute macro, so make sure that the **Relative Reference** button on the *Stop Recording* toolbar is not pressed.
If you wanted to record a relative macro, you would press this button first, before making any other changes you wanted to include in the macro.

6) Apply the following formatting changes:

- Add a horizontal split below row *1*.

- Add a vertical split to the right of column *B*.

- Select **Window | Freeze**.

- Format the text in row *1* as dark blue italics.

- Add a background fill of pale yellow to the cells in row *1*.

- Format the cells in column *A* as dates, selecting 14-Mar-98 from the *Type* area on the **Number** tab of the *Format Cells* dialog box.

7) Select **Tools | Macro | Stop recording**.
– or –
Stop Recording button
Click the **Stop recording** button on the *Stop Recording* toolbar.

8) Save your workbook when you are done.

Running macros

Next, you will learn how to run your saved macro on the *INDOOR* and *OUTDOOR* worksheets, and in a matter of seconds you will have a perfectly consistent set of formatted query results.

In the next exercise, you will run your macro from the *Macro* dialog box and by using the shortcut you defined when recording the macro.

Exercise 10.2: Running a macro

1) Go to the *INDOOR* worksheet of MFPF_ORD.XLS.

2) Select **Tools | Macro | Macros ...** .
The *Macro* dialog box opens.
This dialog box lists all of the macros saved in the current workbook.

3) Select the macro called *format_worksheet* and click **Run**.

4) Go to the *OUTDOOR* worksheet.
   Press **Ctrl** and **d** to run the macro using the shortcut you defined when you created it.

5) Save your workbook when you are done.

All three worksheets are now formatted identically thanks to your macro.

Adding macros to a toolbar

You can add a custom toolbar button to any of Excel's toolbars and assign any command, including a recorded macro, to the new toolbar button.

The toolbar button will always appear on the toolbar, no matter what workbook you are editing. If you click the button when you are editing a different workbook, Excel will open the workbook where the macro is saved in order to run it.

Mrs Murphy wants you to create several more worksheets containing the results of the MFPF_Q1.DQY query, with different sort and filter requirements on each. She wants to have all of the query results formatted in the same way. You decide to add a button to the *Formatting* toolbar so that you can run your macro in one click in future.

In the next exercise, you will add a new button to the *Formatting* toolbar, and assign your macro to that button.

Exercise 10.3: Assigning a macro to a toolbar button

1) Go to any worksheet in MFPF_ORD.XLS.

2) Select **View | Toolbars | Customize ...** .
   The *Customize* dialog box opens.

3) Go to the **Commands** tab of the *Customize* dialog box.

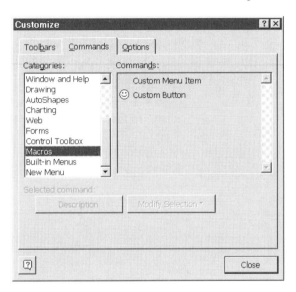

4) In the *Categories* area, select *Macros*.

5) Click the *Custom Button* option in the *Commands* area, and drag it to the *Formatting* toolbar.

6) Right-click the new toolbar button and select *Assign Macro* from the shortcut menu that opens.
   The *Assign Macro* dialog box opens.

7) In the *Macro name* area, select *format_worksheet*, and click **OK**.

8) Click **Close**.
   Your toolbar button now appears on the *Formatting* toolbar.
   Whenever you click it, it will run your recorded macro.

9) Save and close your workbook when you are done.

Over to you: optional

Next, you will use your new toolbar button to apply formatting to query results in a new workbook.

■ Create a new workbook, run the saved query MFPF_Q1.DQY, and click the toolbar button to run your formatting macro. Close the new workbook without saving when you are done.

Chapter summary

A macro is a custom command defined to perform a series of specific actions in the same way and in the same order every time the macro is run.

An absolute macro is one that performs the exact same set of actions on the exact same cell or cell range whenever it is run.

A relative macro performs the set of recorded actions relative to the cell or cell range selected when you run the macro.

You can define a shortcut when you are recording your macro and use that shortcut to run your macro. You can also add a custom toolbar button to any Excel toolbar and assign your macro to that new toolbar button.

11

Using Reference and Mathematical Functions

Up to now, you have done a lot of work setting up your Excel spreadsheets and adding raw data to them. Now you can start to generate some figures for MFPF's incoming revenue and outgoing expenses in the MFPF_FINANCE.XLS workbook.

In this chapter, you will use some of Excel's mathematical functions and commands to generate these numbers.

You will also use reference functions and learn how to nest functions.

New skills

At the end of this chapter you should be able to:

- Use HLOOKUP and VLOOKUP reference functions
- Use the **Subtotals** command
- Create a 3D sum function
- Use the SUMIF mathematical function
- Use the ROUND mathematical function

New words

There are no new words in this chapter.

Maths with Paste Special

In Chapter 6 you learned that you can use Excel's **Paste Special** command to combine copied numerical data with numerical data in a destination cell or cell range using simple mathematical functions. Now you will use this functionality to calculate sales revenue and materials costs for the products sold by MFPF over the year.

The *INCOMING* worksheet of MFPF_FINANCE.XLS has an empty column, *Products*, where you will put figures for incoming revenue from product sales.

To work out these figures, you will combine the sales figures you calculated in Chapter 7 with the data you imported from PRICES.TXT in Chapter 3. Both of these sets of numbers are on the *SALES TOTALS* worksheet of MFPF_FINANCE.XLS.

In the next exercise, you will create a copy of the named cell range *SALES*, and combine the data in the cell range with the prices in the *Sell for* row to work out the revenue generated by sales of each product each month.

Exercise 11.1: Multiplying numbers using Paste Special

1) Open MFPF_FINANCE.XLS and go to the cell range named *SALES*.

2) Copy the *SALES* cell range, and paste the data to a new cell range starting in cell *A18* on the *SALES TOTALS* worksheet.

3) Name the new cell range *REVENUE*.

4) Copy the product price data in cells *B16:H16*.

5) Select the cell range *B19:H30*.

6) Select **Edit | Paste Special**.
   The *Paste Special* dialog box opens.

7) In the *Paste* area, select *Values*.
   In the *Operation* area, select *Multiply*.
   Click **OK**.

8) Save your workbook.

The *REVENUE* cell range now indicates the total money earned by MFPF by selling each product type each month.

Now that you know how much was earned by selling each product type each month, you will calculate the total revenue for the month by adding all of these figures up.

- Using the SUM function, which you learned about in ECDL 3, add up the revenue figures for all product types each month.

- Copy and paste the final revenue figures for each month into the *Products* column on the INCOMING worksheet.

Next, you will work out how much was spent on the materials needed to make the ordered furniture each month, and add those figures to the *Materials* column on the OUTGOING worksheet.

- Create another copy of the *SALES* range on the SALES TOTALS worksheet.

- Combine the data in the new cell range with the figures in the *Materials* row to calculate materials costs for each furniture type each month.

- Calculate the monthly total for materials purchases, and copy and paste the final figures to the *Materials* column on the OUTGOING worksheet.

Save your workbook when you are done.

Reference functions

There are only two more sets of figures left to calculate to complete the records on the INCOMING and OUTGOING worksheets: revenue from delivery charges, and expenditure on petrol while making the deliveries.

To calculate these figures, you will use the data in DELIVERIES.XLS. The CHARGES worksheet indicates how far away each customer is, and what delivery charge they pay for each order. The DELIVERIES worksheet lists the date of each delivery, and the customer to which the delivery was made.

You will add a third column to the DELIVERIES worksheet, which shows the delivery charge paid for each order.

To calculate this value, you will need to check which customer each row in the *DELIVERIES* worksheet refers to, and then look up the delivery charge for that customer on the *CHARGES* worksheet.

To do this, you will use a reference function, VLOOKUP.

VLOOKUP

VLOOKUP is an Excel function that checks a cell range for a row starting with a specified value, and returns the value in a specified column of that row.

The reference function VLOOKUP has the following format:

=VLOOKUP(Lookup_value, Table_array, Col_index_num, Range_lookup)	
Lookup_value	The value to look for in the first column of the *Table_array*.
Table_array	The cell range to look at. Entries in the *Table_array* must be sorted by the first column in ascending order if you specify a value of *1* for *Range_lookup*.
Col_index_num	The number (not letter) for the column in the table array that contains the value you want returned.
Range_lookup	*1 (TRUE)* or *0 (FALSE)*. If you leave this value blank, 0 is used by default. If *Range_lookup* is *1*, then if the *Lookup_value* is not found, the row starting with the closest value less than the *Lookup_value* is used instead. This is why the entries in the *Table_array* must be sorted by the first column in ascending order. If *Range_lookup* is *0*, then an error will be given if an exact match to your *Lookup_value* is not found in the first column of the *Table_array*.

Note: The parts of the function in the brackets are called parameters. They should always be separated by commas.

Some parameters are optional, and you do not have to specify a value for them. If you do not specify a value for a parameter, you should include a blank space instead of that parameter, and separate it from the other parameter values using commas – this tells Excel that the next value given is for the next parameter and not for the one you are skipping. If an optional parameter comes at the end of the parameter list, you can simply leave it out.

In the next exercise, you will use the VLOOKUP function to find the corresponding *Delivery charge* in column *C* on the *CHARGES* worksheet for the *CompanyName* in column *B* of every record on the *DELIVERIES* worksheet.

Exercise 11.2: Using VLOOKUP

1) Open DELIVERIES.XLS and go to the *DELIVERIES* worksheet.

2) Label column *C Delivery charge*.

3) In cell *C2* on the *DELIVERIES* worksheet, enter the following formula:
   =VLOOKUP(B2,CHARGES!$A$1:$C$7,3)
   to find the value in the third column of the table array on the *CHARGES* worksheet for the company listed in cell *B2* of the *DELIVERIES* worksheet.

4) Copy the formula to the other cells in column *C*.

   Column *C* now contains the charge for each delivery listed.

   Note: The relative *B2* cell reference is updated to reflect the appropriate row in the copied formulae, but the absolute references used to define the table array mean that the same cell range on the *CHARGES* worksheet is used in each formula.

Over to you: mandatory

Next, you will work out how much was spent on petrol for each delivery.

- Label column *D* on the *DELIVERIES* worksheet *Petrol*.
- In cell *D2*, enter a formula that multiplies the distance to the customer listed in cell *B2* for each delivery by 2 to get the round-trip distance, and then by £0.06 (the average cost Mr Murphy pays for petrol per km). Use a VLOOKUP function to find the distance to the customer in the same table array used in the previous exercise.

HLOOKUP

A similar function to VLOOKUP, called HLOOKUP, checks a cell range for a column starting with a specified value, and returns the value in a specified row of that column.

The reference function HLOOKUP has the following format:

=HLOOKUP(Lookup_value, Table_array, Col_index_num, Range_lookup)	
Lookup_value	The value to look for in the first row of the *Table_array*.
Table_array	The cell range to look at. Entries in the *Table_array* must be sorted by the first row in ascending order if you specify a value of *1* for *Range_lookup*.
Row_index_num	The number for the row in the table array that contains the value you want returned.
Range_lookup	*1 (TRUE)* or *0 (FALSE)*. If you leave this value blank, 0 is used by default. If *Range_lookup* is *1*, then if the *Lookup_value* is not found, the column starting with the closest value less than the *Lookup_value* is used instead. This is why the entries in the *Table_array* must be sorted by the first row in ascending order. If *Range_lookup* is *0*, then an error will be given if an exact match to your *Lookup_value* is not found in the first row of the *Table_array*.

Next, you will work out the delivery charge for each order using a transposed table array and HLOOKUP.

Chapter 11: Using Reference and Mathematical Functions

Exercise 11.3: Using HLOOKUP

1) Go to the *CHARGES* worksheet of DELIVERIES.XLS.

2) Copy the cell range *A1:C7.*

3) Insert a new worksheet into the workbook and name it *CHARGES2*.

4) Use **Paste Special**'s *Transpose* option to paste the values from the copied data to cell rage *A1:G3*.

5) In cell *E2* on the *DELIVERIES* worksheet, enter the following formula:
   =HLOOKUP(B2,CHARGES2!$A$1:$G$3,3)
   to find the value in the third fow of the table array on the *CHARGES2* worksheet for the company listed in cell *B2* of the *DELIVERIES* worksheet.

6) Copy the formula to the other cells in column *E*.

The numbers in column *E* should be the same as those in column *C*.

Subtotalling

Now you know the charge and the cost of petrol for each delivery. Next, you will work out what the monthly total for each one is, using Excel's **Subtotals** command.

The **Subtotals** command allows you to create subtotals of the values in specified columns in a sorted list. Excel looks for changes in the values in specified sorted columns to identify the end of a group, and adds a subtotal at that point.

In the next exercise, you will sort the data on the *DELIVERIES* worksheet of DELIVERIES.XLS by month, and calculate monthly subtotals for delivery charges and petrol.

Before calculating monthly subtotals, you will change the format of the entries in the *DeliveryDate* column to show the month and year only, otherwise each change in the day of the month will be identified as the end of a group, and you will calculate subtotals for each day instead of for each month.

Exercise 11.4: Calculating subtotals

1) Go to the *DELIVERIES* worksheet of DELIVERIES.XLS and select column *A*.

2) Select **Format | Cells ... **.
   – or –
   Click the **Format Cells** button on the *Formatting* toolbar.
   The *Format Cells* dialog box opens.

3) Click the **Number** tab.

4) In the *Category* area, select *Date*, and in the *Type* area, select *Mar-98*.
   This will format the dates to show only their month and year components.
   Click **OK**.

5) Select columns *A* to *D*, and then select **Data | Subtotals ... **.
   The *Subtotal* dialog box opens.

6) In the *At each change in* field, select *DeliveryDate*.
   In the *Use function* field, select *Sum*.
   In the *Add subtotal to* area, check the boxes beside *Delivery Charge* and *Petrol*
   Your dialog box should now look like this:

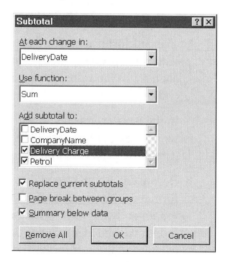

Click **OK**.

Excel calculates subtotals for the specified columns, and adds them to your worksheet.

Outline Area

7) Click the '-' symbols in the *Outline* area to hide the record rows and show only the subtotal results.

8) Save your workbook when you are done.

Over to you: mandatory

Next, you will add the subtotals for each month to MFPF_FINANCE.XLS.

- Using **Copy** and **Paste Special**, copy the monthly revenue from deliveries and the monthly petrol expenses to the spaces left for them on the *INCOMING* and *OUTGOING* worksheets of MFPF_FINANCE.XLS. Save both workbooks when you are done, and close DELIVERIES.XLS.

  Note: You will have to copy each figure individually instead of copying the cell range. If you try to copy the cell range containing the results, you will also copy the cells in the hidden rows.

3D sum

In ECDL 3, you learned how to use the SUM function to add up the values in a 2D cell range on a worksheet. You can also use the SUM function to sum in three dimensions, across a series of worksheets, where the numbers you want to add up appear in the same cell or cell range on each worksheet.

A 3D sum function has the following format:

=SUM(First_sheet:Last_sheet!Cell)	
First_sheet	The first worksheet in the 3D range.
Last_sheet	The last worksheet in the 3D range.
Cell	The cell or cell range on all of the worksheets in the specified range that contains the values you want to sum.

On the *INCOMING* and *OUTGOING* worksheets of MFPF_FINANCE.XLS, the total amounts of money each year that are earned by the business and paid out by the business are calculated in cell *C15*.

In the next exercise, you will add a 3D sum to the *PROFIT* worksheet, which adds up the values that appear in cell *C15* on each sheet.

Exercise 11.5: Creating a 3D sum

1) Go to the *PROFIT* worksheet of MFPF_FINANCE.XLS.

2) Select cell *C15*.

Autosum button   3) Click the **Autosum** button on the *Standard* toolbar.

4) Go to the *INCOMING* worksheet and select cell *C15*.

5) Hold down the **Shift** key and click the tab for the *OUTGOING* worksheet.

6) Press **Enter**.

7) Save your workbook when you are done.

The total calculated by adding together the values in cell *C15* on each of the worksheets is now displayed in cell *C15* on the *PROFIT* worksheet.

SUMIF

You can specify that you want to sum data only if they satisfy certain criteria using Excel's SUMIF function.

The mathematical function SUMIF has the following format:

=SUMIF(Range_to_eval, Criteria, Sum_range)	
Range_to_eval	The range of cells to check against your criteria.
Criteria	The tests to perform to see whether to include the data in the sum.
Sum_range	The range of cells containing the data you want to sum. If you do not specify a *Sum_range*, the values in the *Range_to_eval* will be summed instead. There should be a one-to-one correspondence between cells in the *Range_to_eval* and *Sum_range*.

Note: Criteria are enclosed in quotation marks, can be any comparisons using the expressions <, >, =, <= (which means less than or equal to) or >= (which means greater than or equal to), and can include cell references as well as numeric and text values.

MFPF currently requires a minimum order of eight for garden chairs. Mr Murphy is thinking about increasing this number to 12. He has asked you to look at last year's figures and work out how many chairs would have been sold if MFPF had refused to fill orders for less than 12 chairs at a time.

In the next exercise, you will calculate how many chairs were sold last year in total, and how many of them were sold in orders for 12 or more chairs.

Exercise 11.6: Using the SUMIF function

1) Open MFPF_ORD.XLS and go to the *COMPLETE* worksheet.

2) In cell *I56*, below the column giving order numbers for garden chairs, enter the formula =*SUM(I2:I55)*.

3) In cell *I57* enter the formula =*SUMIF(I2:I55, ">=12")*.

The number in cell *I57* is smaller than the number in *I56*, because only those orders for 12 or more chairs were included in the sum.

Next, check how many garden tables would have been sold if no order for less than three tables at a time was filled. Save and close the workbook when you are done.

SUMPOSITIVE

As you know, ECDL is a vendor-independent certification. One of the Advanced Spreadsheets syllabus requirements is to know about SUMPOSITIVE. SUMPOSITIVE is a Lotus 1-2-3 function that sums only the positive values in a cell range. You can use Excel's SUMIF function to do the same job using the formula =*SUMIF(Range_to_eval, ">0", Sum_range)*.

ROUND

Occasionally, you will want to round numbers on a spreadsheet to a particular number of decimal places. Excel's ROUND function allows you to specify any number of digits before or after the decimal point to which you can round the number.

The mathematical function ROUND has the following format:

=ROUND(Number, Num_digits)	
Number	The number you want to round.
Num_digits	The number of digits before or after the decimal point to round to. A negative number indicates a position to the left of the decimal point, and a positive number indicates a position to the right.

Mrs Murphy has asked you to provide her with a list of the monthly profits on the *PROFIT* worksheet of MFPF_FINANCE.XLS, with each value rounded to the nearest £100.

In the next exercise, you will add a column to the *PROFIT* worksheet, which shows rounded profit figures for each month.

Exercise 11.7: Using the ROUND function

1) Open MFPF_FINANCE.XLS and go to the *PROFIT* worksheet.

2) Label column *E* Rounded Profit.

3) In cell *E2*, enter the formula =*ROUND(D2, –2)*.

4) Copy the formula to the cells *E3:E13*.

Column *E* now shows the profits for each month of the year rounded to the nearest £100.

D	E
Profit	**Rounded Profit**
£3,482.84	£3,500.00
£1,057.78	£1,100.00
£605.32	£600.00
£465.94	£500.00
£3,060.26	£3,100.00
£2,590.76	£2,600.00
£3,695.02	£3,700.00
£2,997.06	£3,000.00
£508.74	£500.00
£185.98	£200.00
£1,648.84	£1,600.00
£598.00	£600.00

Nesting

In the previous exercise, you used the ROUND function to manipulate a number generated by a SUM function. You could have combined both functions in a single formula by nesting them.

If you use one function as an argument in another function, then the first function is nested in the second.

You can nest up to seven functions inside a function.

In the next exercise, you will create a nested function to calculate the profit figure for a month and round it to the nearest £100.

Exercise 11.8: Nesting functions

1) Open MFPF_FINANCE.XLS and go to the *PROFIT* worksheet.

2) Label column *F Rounded Profit (using nesting)*.

3) In cell *F2*, enter *=ROUND(SUM(B2:C2),_2)*.
   This formula first calculates the sum of the values in the cells in the cell range *B2:C2*, and then applies the ROUND function to show the result rounded to the nearest hundreds value.

4) Copy the formula to cells *F3:F13*.

The results in column *F* are identical to those in column *E* and were achieved using just one formula.

When you are done, save and close your workbook.

Chapter summary

VLOOKUP is an Excel function that checks a cell range for a row starting with a specified value, and returns the value in a specified column of that row.

HLOOKUP is an Excel function that checks a cell range for a column starting with a specified value, and returns the value in a specified row of that column.

The **Subtotals** command allows you to create subtotals of values in a sorted list. Excel looks for changes in the values in one specified column to identify the end of a group, and creates a subtotal at that point.

You can use the SUM function to sum in three dimensions, across a series of worksheets, where the numbers you want to add up appear in the same cell or cell range on each worksheet.

You can specify that you want to include data in a calculation only if they satisfy certain criteria, using the SUMIF function.

The ROUND function allows you to specify any number of digits before or after the decimal point to which the number is to be rounded.

You can combine a number of functions in a single formula by nesting them inside one another, using parentheses.

12

Customizing Charts

In this chapter

In ECDL 3 you learned how to create charts in Excel, and how to make simple changes to them.

In this chapter you will learn how to make more advanced changes to charts after you have added them.

New skills

At the end of this chapter you should be able to:

- Delete a data series from a chart
- Change the angle of pie-chart slices
- Explode all the segments in a pie chart
- Format the text or numbers on a chart axis
- Reposition chart titles, legends and data labels
- Widen the gap between columns or bars in a chart
- Insert an image into a chart

New words

There are no new words in this chapter.

Deleting a data series from a chart

Sometimes, you may find that after you have created a chart you need to remove a particular data series. Maybe one data series dominates the chart, making it difficult to see the others. Maybe you accidentally included values for a salesperson who deals with a different geographical area from the one covered by the chart.

You could delete your chart, reselect the source data, and generate a new chart that shows only the relevant data series.

But Excel allows you to edit the chart directly and remove the data series there, preserving any other changes you have made in the meantime.

Mrs Murphy has asked you to generate a chart that shows the sales of each product each month over the year.

In the next exercise, you will create the chart, and add it to a new worksheet in MFPF_FINANCE.XLS.

Exercise 12.1: Creating a column chart

1) Open MFPF_FINANCE.XLS and select the cell range named *SALES*.

2) Select **Insert | Chart ...** .
   – or –
   Click the **Chart Wizard** button on the *Standard* toolbar.
   The *Chart Wizard* dialog box appears.

3) In the *Chart type* area, select *Column*.
   In the *Chart sub-type* area, select *Clustered column with a 3-D visual effect*.

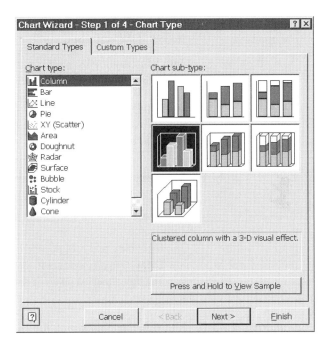

4) Click **Next** until you get to the last screen in the *Chart Wizard: Chart Location*.

5) Select *Add as new sheet*, and click **Finish**.
Your chart is created and added to a new worksheet named *Chart1*. Your chart should look like this:

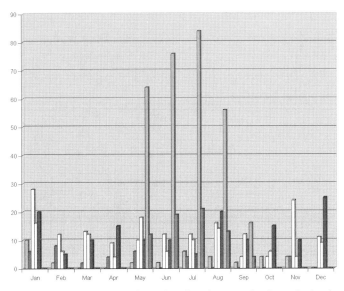

There is a trend for a lot of garden furniture to be bought in the summer months. Because of these high summer sales, the data series for garden chairs swamps the rest of the data in the chart.

The fact that there are up to seven columns in each cluster also makes it difficult to distinguish one column from another.

Mrs Murphy looks at the chart, and asks you to change it to show data for sales of bedroom furniture only.

In the next exercise, you will begin to delete data series from the chart you already generated, instead of regenerating the chart with the required data only.

Exercise 12.2: Deleting a data series from a chart

1) Click any data point (i.e., column) in the *Garden Chair* data series to select the whole data series, and press the **Delete** key.
    – or –
    Right-click any data point in the *Garden Chair* data series and select **Clear** from the shortcut menu that appears.
    The data series is deleted from the chart.

Over to you: mandatory

Remove the data series for *Garden Table*, *Kitchen Organizer* and *Coffee Table* in the same way.

Your chart now contains three columns in each cluster of data points. It is much easier to read than the original graph.

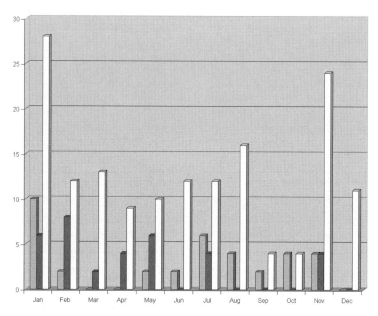

Save the workbook when you are done.

Modifying the chart type for a data series

MFPF have a black-and-white printer. It will still be difficult to distinguish which column represents which product when the chart is printed. Excel allows you to represent each data series in a chart in a different chart type. You decide to apply a different chart type to each data series in your chart to make the distinction clearer.

In the next exercise, you will change the chart type for the *Wardrobe* data series to *Cylinder*.

Exercise 12.3: Changing the chart type for a data series

1) Right-click the *Wardrobe* data series, and select **Chart Type** from the shortcut menu that opens.
   The *Chart Type* dialog box appears.

2) In the *Chart type* area, select *Cylinder*.

3) In the *Options* area, select *Apply to selection* to change the chart type for the selected data series only.

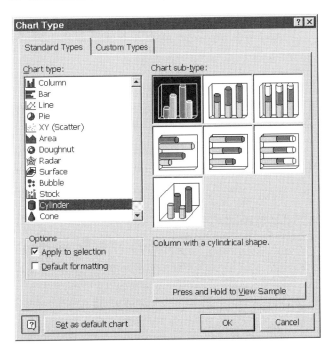

4) Click **OK**.

Next, change the chart type for the *Chest of Drawers* data series to *Cone* and save the workbook when you are done.

Your chart should now look like this:

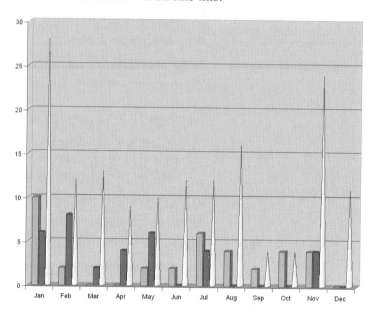

Formatting chart axes

You can change the font attributes for any text that appears in your chart.

You decide to make some more changes to the chart to improve the legibility of the data shown.

In the next exercise, you will change the font attributes of the text on the axes of the chart.

Exercise 12.4: Formatting chart axes

1) Right-click the horizontal axis showing the months of the year to select it.
   A small white square appears at each end of the axis line when it is selected.

2) Select **Format Axis** from the shortcut menu that appears.
   The *Format Axis* dialog box opens.

3) Click the **Font** tab.

4) Assign the following font settings:

- *Font: Verdana*
- *Size: 11*
- *Color: Dark blue*

5) Click **OK**.
Your font format changes are applied to the text on the axis.

Over to you: mandatory

Format the numbers on the vertical axis to appear with the same font settings.

Widening the gaps between columns in a chart

Excel adds a certain amount of space between the columns in a chart by default. You can change how much space appears between columns if you want.

Mrs Murphy asks you to change your chart to a 2D column representation, and to add extra space between the column clusters and between the columns in each cluster to make it easier to read the chart.

In the next exercise, you will change the chart type for all the data series, and add extra space between the columns in each cluster and between the individual clusters.

Exercise 12.5: Widening the gaps between columns in a 2D chart

1) Right-click any data series in your chart, and select **Chart Type** from the shortcut menu that opens.
The *Chart Type* dialog box appears.

2) In the *Chart type* area, select *Column*.

3) Make sure that the check box beside *Apply to selection* is unchecked.

4) Click **OK**.
The chart is reformatted so that all data series are 2D columns.

5) Right-click any data series, and select **Format Data Series** from the shortcut menu that opens.
The *Format Data Series* dialog box opens.

6) Click the **Options** tab.

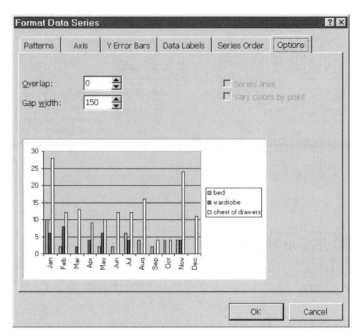

7) In the *Overlap* field, enter *–50*, either by entering the number in the box, or by using the up/down arrows to the right of the box to change the value.
Overlap refers to the size of the gap between the columns in each cluster.
In the *Gap width* field, enter *400*.
Gap width refers to the gap between adjacent clusters.
The graph on the lower half of the tab changes to show the effect of your changes.

8) Click **OK**.
Extra space is added between the columns.

Inserting a picture in a chart

Excel allows you to add a graphic to the plot area, the chart area, a data series, or a data point in your chart.

You decide to change the default background of the plot area to the MFPF logo.

In the next exercise, you will add the company logo as a background to the chart area.

Exercise 12.6: Adding a graphic to a chart

1) Right-click the plot area and select **Format Plot Area** from the shortcut menu that opens.
The *Format Plot Area* dialog box opens.

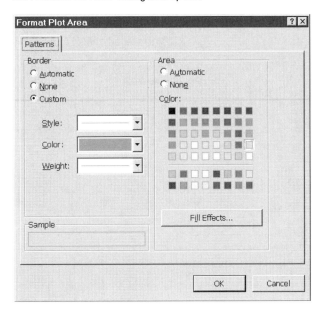

2) Click **Fill Effects ... .**
The *Fill Effects* dialog box opens.

3) Click the **Picture** tab.

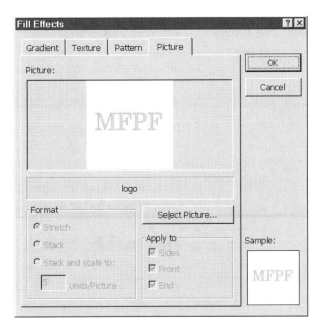

4) Click **Select Picture ...** .
   The *Select Picture* dialog box opens.

5) Select the file LOGO.GIF from your working folder, and click **Insert**.

6) Click **OK**.

7) Click **OK**.
   Your chart should now look like this:

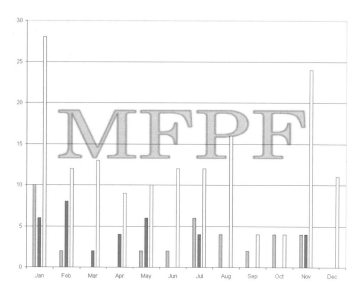

8) Save your workbook when you are done.

Changing the angle of slices in a pie chart

When you insert a pie chart, the order of the slices is determined by the order of the values in the worksheet cells used to generate the chart. While you cannot change the order the slices appear in in the chart, you can rotate a pie chart to change the angle at which the first slice appears relative to the 12 o'clock position.

July was the busiest month for MFPF. Mrs Murphy has asked you to generate a pie chart showing the breakdown of sales in that month.

In the next exercise, you will generate a pie chart showing the sales of each furniture type for the month of July.

Exercise 12.7: Creating a pie chart

1) Go to the *SALES TOTALS* worksheet of MFPF_FINANCE.XLS.

2) Select the non-adjacent cell ranges *A1:H1* and *A8:H8*.

3) Select **Insert | Chart ...** .
   – or –
   Click the **Chart Wizard** button on the *Standard* toolbar.
   The *Chart Wizard* opens.

4) In the *Chart type* area, select *Pie*.

5) Click **Next** until you get to the last screen in the *Chart Wizard: Chart Location*.

6) Select *Add as new sheet*, and click **Finish**.
   Your chart is created and added on to a new worksheet named *Chart2*.

Garden chairs make up most of the sales. Mrs Murphy would like the pie slice representing garden chairs to be the last one in the pie, ending at the 12 o'clock position.

In the next exercise, you will change the angle of the pie chart, so that the pie slice for garden chairs appears last. You will also add data labels to each slice to show how many units of furniture each one represents.

Exercise 12.8: Changing the angle of slices in a pie chart

1) Right-click the pie chart and select **Format Data Series** from the shortcut menu that opens.
   The *Format Data Series* dialog box opens.

2) Click the **Options** tab.

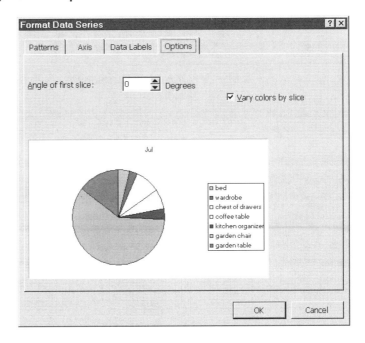

3) Change the value in the *Angle of first slice* box to *54*, either by entering the number in the box, or by using the up/down arrows to the right of the box to change the value.
If you use the up/down arrows to change the angle, you can see the pie chart rotate in the preview area on this screen.

4) Click the **Data Labels** tab.

5) In the *Data labels* area, select *Show values*.

6) Click **OK**.
Your pie chart is rotated as specified on the **Options** tab, and data labels have been added to each slice, showing the number of units of each furniture type sold.

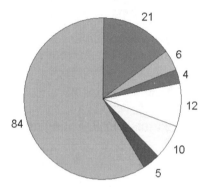

Exploding all the slices in a pie chart

In ECDL 3, you learned how to explode individual slices in a pie to make them easier to see. There is also a pie-chart subtype called *Exploded Pie*, in which all of the slices of the pie chart are exploded.

It is easier to change the chart subtype than to explode each slice individually.

In the next exercise, you will change the chart subtype from *Pie* to *Exploded Pie*, so that you can see the smaller slices more clearly.

Exercise 12.9: Changing the chart type

1) Right-click the pie chart, and select **Chart Type** from the shortcut menu that opens.
The *Chart Type* dialog box appears.

2) *Pie* is already selected in the *Chart type* area.
In the *Chart sub-type* area, select *Exploded pie*.

3) Click **OK**.
Your chart is now an exploded pie chart

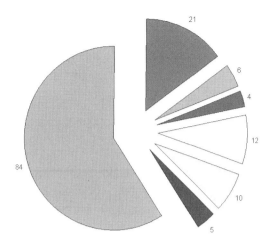

Repositioning chart elements

The chart title, legend and data labels are added to default positions in a chart in Excel. If you would prefer to see them in different positions, you can select any one of them and drag it to any other position on the chart that you like.

In the next exercise, you will reposition the title of the pie chart, so that instead of appearing above the chart, it appears just to the left of it.

Exercise 12.10: Repositioning a chart title

1) Select the chart title, *Jul*, by clicking it once.
   A rectangle of small black boxes appears around the text box when it is selected.

2) Click the border of the text box, and drag it to its new position, just left of the chart.

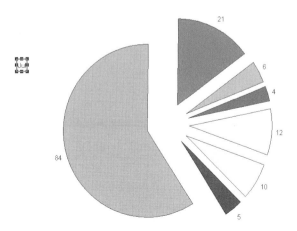

Next, you will move some other chart elements.

■ Move the legend, by default located in a box to the right of the chart, to just below the chart title on the left of the chart.

■ Drag the data labels for each pie slice on to the relevant slice.

When you are done, save and close MFPF_FINANCE.XLS.

Chapter summary

You can make changes to a chart after it has been created. You can remove individual data series, or represent each data series in a chart by a different chart type.

You can change the font attributes for any text in your chart.

You can change how much space appears between columns in a column chart, or rotate a pie chart to change the angle at which the first slice appears relative to the 12 o'clock position.

You can add graphics to the plot area, the chart area, data series, and data points in your chart.

You can move chart elements to new positions if you are not happy with the default layout.

13

Using Statistical and Database Functions

In this chapter

Sometimes, you will want to count the number of cells in a range that contain a particular type of data, although you don't want to do anything with the values in the cells.

In this chapter you will learn how to count the number of cells in a range that contains a certain type of value or that satisfy specified criteria.

You will also learn about Excel 'databases', and find out how to count fields and sum the values they contain using criteria to specify which fields to include. You will also learn how to find minimum and maximum values in Excel database fields.

New skills

At the end of this chapter you should be able to:

- Use the COUNT function
- Use the COUNTA function
- Use the COUNTIF function
- Use the DSUM function
- Use the DMIN and DMAX functions
- Use the DCOUNT function

New words

At the end of this chapter you should be able to explain the following term:

- Excel database

Statistical functions

The statistical functions you will learn about in this chapter are used to count the number of cells in a cell range that contain a particular type of data, or data that satisfy specified criteria.

COUNT

COUNT is an Excel function that looks at a list of values and calculates how many of them are numeric. Blanks and text values are disregarded.

The statistical function COUNT has the following format:

COUNT(Value1, Value2, ...)	
Value1, Value2, ...	A list of values or a cell range containing the data elements to count. Only the numeric values are counted.

Mr Murphy asks you to calculate exactly how many orders were made in the year.

You could calculate the total number of orders by looking at the row number of the first entry and the row number of the last, and subtracting one from the other. But using COUNT, you can simply tell Excel to look at any of the columns that contain order numbers and count how many entries in that range are numbers.

In the next exercise, you will use COUNT to calculate how many of the cells in column *J* contain numeric values and thereby determine how many orders were made.

> **Note:** If you completed the optional SUMIF exercise on page 100, you should delete the SUM and SUMIF formulae you added in column *J* of the *COMPLETE* worksheet in MFPF_ORD.XLS. The results of these formulae are numeric values and would be counted by the functions in the following exercises.

Exercise 13.1: Using COUNT

1) Open MFPF_ORD.XLS and go to the *COMPLETE* worksheet.

2) In cell *N2*, enter the formula *=COUNT(J:J)* to count all the rows in column *J* that contain a number.
   The answer is 54.
   Cell *J1*, which contains label text, and the blank cells in the column were not counted.

3) Save your workbook when you are done.

COUNTA

COUNTA is an Excel function that looks at a list of values and counts how many of them are non-blank. Any numeric or textual value will add to the count total.

COUNTA is the Excel function equivalent to Lotus 1-2-3's PURECOUNT.

The statistical function COUNTA has the following format:

COUNTA(Value1, Value2, ...)	
Value1, Value2, ...	A list of values or a cell range containing the data elements to count. All non-blank values are counted.

In the next exercise, you will count how many cells in column *J* of the *COMPLETE* worksheet of MFPF_ORD.XLS contain values.

Exercise 13.2: Using COUNTA

1) Go to the *COMPLETE* worksheet of MFPF_ORD.XLS.

2) In cell *N3*, enter the formula *=COUNTA(J:J)*.
   The answer is 55.
   Cell *J1* contains text, so it was included in the count, but the blank cells in the column were ignored again.

3) Save your workbook when you are done.

COUNTIF

COUNTIF is an Excel function that looks at a list of values, and calculates how many of them satisfy specified criteria.

The statistical function COUNTIF has the following format:

COUNTIF(Range, Criteria)	
Range	The cell range containing the values to be counted.
Criteria	The criteria the value in a cell must satisfy for that cell to be included in the count.

Earlier, you used SUMIF to see how many chairs MFPF would have sold if no orders for fewer than 12 at a time had been filled. How many actual orders would not have been filled?

In the next exercise, you will use COUNTIF to find the number of values in the *Chairs* column on the *COMPLETE* worksheet of MFPF_ORD.XLS that are lower than 12.

Exercise 13.3: Using COUNTIF

1) Open MFPF_ORD.XLS and go to the *COMPLETE* worksheet.

2) In cell *I58*, enter the formula *=COUNTIF(I2:I55,"<12")*. There were 38 occasions on which fewer than 12 chairs were ordered.

3) Save your workbook when you are done.

Database functions

The 'database' referred to in the term 'database function' is not an external one, such as Microsoft Access. It is a table or list of related data in an Excel spreadsheet.

> **Excel database**
>
> *An Excel database is a table or list of related data in an Excel spreadsheet that can be treated as a database of records.*

Excel database functions are used to make calculations based on the data in specific fields of a table or list row, where the row satisfies specified criteria.

DSUM

DSUM is an Excel function that looks at a list or table of values, finds the rows that satisfy specified criteria, and adds up the values in a specified column of those rows.

The database function DSUM has the following format:

=DSUM(Database, Field, Criteria)	
Database	The cell range you will use as your database for the purposes of this calculation.
Field	The number (not letter) for the column that contains the values you want to sum.
Criteria	The criteria that must be satisfied for the row values to be included in the sum. Criteria for database functions are specified as a range of cell pairs, where one cell contains a column name and the cell below it contains the value that should appear in that column. Each of the criteria specified must be satisfied for the row values to be included in the sum.

In the next exercise, you will use the DSUM function to calculate the total number of garden chairs ordered by the Cullenstown Garden Centre, using the data on the *COMPLETE* worksheet of MFPF_ORD.XLS as your database.

The cell range containing the query results you will use as your database was automatically given the custom name of *MFPF_Q1* when you imported the data. You will use that name to identify the cell range in the function.

Exercise 13.4: Using DSUM

1) Go to the *COMPLETE* worksheet of MFPF_ORD.XLS.

2) Enter the label *CompanyName* (with no spaces) in cell *N6*.
Enter the value *Cullenstown Garden Centre* in cell *N7*.
This is the criterion you will use to find the rows in the database to include in the sum.

3) In cell *N9*, enter the label *Chairs ordered*.

4) In cell *O9*, enter the formula *=DSUM(MFPF_Q1,9,N6:N7)*.
108 chairs were ordered in the year by Cullenstown Garden Centre.

DMIN

DMIN is an Excel function that looks at a list or table of values, finds the rows that satisfy specified criteria, and determines the minimum value in a specified column of those rows.

The database function DMIN has the following format:

=DMIN(Database, Field, Criteria)	
Database	The cell range you will use as your database for the purposes of this calculation.
Field	The number of the column in which you want to find the minimum value.
Criteria	The cell range containing the criteria for the rows to include.

In the next exercise, you will use the DMIN function to find the smallest order for garden chairs placed by the Cullenstown Garden Centre.

Exercise 13.5: Using DMIN

1) Open MFPF_ORD.XLS, and go to the *COMPLETE* worksheet.

2) In cell *N10*, enter the label *Smallest chair order.*

3) In cell *O10*, enter the formula *=DMIN(MFPF_Q1,9,N6:N7)*.
The smallest order was for eight chairs.

DMAX

DMAX is an Excel function that looks at a list or table of values, finds the rows that satisfy specified criteria, and determines the maximum value in a specified column of those rows.

The database function DMAX has the following format:

=DMAX(Database, Field, Criteria)	
Database	The cell range you will use as your database for the purposes of this calculation.
Field	The number of the column in which you want to find the maximum value.
Criteria	The cell range containing the criteria for the rows to include.

In the next exercise, you will use the DMAX function to find the largest order for garden chairs placed by the Cullenstown Garden Centre.

Exercise 13.6: Using DMAX

1) Open MFPF_ORD.XLS, and go to the *COMPLETE* worksheet.

2) In cell *N11*, enter the label *Largest chair order.*

3) In cell *O11*, enter the formula =*DMAX(MFPF_Q1,9,N6:N7).*
   The largest order was for 32 chairs.

DCOUNT

DCOUNT is an Excel function that looks at a list or table of values, finds the rows that satisfy specified criteria, and counts them.

The database function DCOUNT has the following format:

=DCOUNT(Database, Field, Criteria)	
Database	The cell range you will use as your database for the purposes of this calculation.
Field	The number of the column that contains the values you want to count.
Criteria	The cell range containing the criteria for the rows to include.

In the next exercise, you will use the DCOUNT function to find how many orders for 12 or more garden chairs were placed by the Cullenstown Garden Centre.

Exercise 13.7: Using DCOUNT

1) Open MFPF_ORD.XLS, and go to the *COMPLETE* worksheet.

2) In cell *O6*, enter the criterion label *Chair*.
   In cell *O7*, enter *>=12*.

3) In cell *N13*, enter the label *12+ chairs*.

4) In cell *O13*, enter the formula *=DCOUNT(MFPF_Q1,9,N6:O7)*.
   This formula tells Excel to count the entries in the ninth column of the *MFPF_Q1* database (named cell range) that match the criteria defined in the cell range *N6:O7*.
   (*N6:N7* specifies the Cullenstown Garden Centre; *O6:O7* specifies 12 or more chairs; N6:O7 combines the two.)
   The result shows that Cullenstown Garden Centre made six orders for 12 or more chairs.

Chapter summary

Excel's COUNT function looks at a list of values, and calculates how many are numeric. Blanks and text values are disregarded.

The COUNTA function calculates how many of the values are non-blank. Any numeric or textual value will add to the count total. COUNTA is the Excel function equivalent of Lotus 1-2-3's PURECOUNT.

The COUNTIF function looks at a list of values, and calculates how many of them satisfy specified criteria.

An Excel database is a table or list of related data in an Excel spreadsheet that can be treated as a database of records.

The database function DSUM looks at a list or table of values, finds the rows that satisfy specified criteria, and adds up the values in a specified column of those rows.

DMIN finds the rows that satisfy specified criteria, and determines the minimum value in a specified column of those rows. Similarly, DMAX determines the maximum value in a specified column.

The DCOUNT function looks at a list or table of values, finds the rows that satisfy specified criteria, and counts them.

14

Using Financial Functions

In this chapter

So far in this book, you have learned about reference, mathematical, statistical and database functions in Excel.

Most of the time, Excel is used to keep track of financial information. Because of this, Excel also includes a set of functions specifically designed to handle financial data. These functions calculate typical accounting figures, such as the future value of a series of investments at a fixed interest rate.

In this chapter, you will learn how to use some of Excel's financial functions.

New skills

At the end of this chapter you should be able to:

- Use the NPV function
- Use the PV function
- Use the FV function
- Use the PMT function
- Use the RATE function

New words

There are no new words in this chapter.

NPV

NPV is an Excel function that calculates the net present value of an investment or debt. This gives the value in today's money of your investment or debt at the end of the investment period.

Because of factors such as inflation and depreciation, an investment you own today may not be worth as much in relative terms in the future.

The financial function NPV has the following format:

=NPV(Rate, Value1, Value2, ...)	
Rate	The discount rate per period of investment (for example, the inflation rate per period).
Value1, Value2, ...	A list of the payments made into the investment (negative numbers), and the income earned on the investment (positive numbers) over the total investment period. The values can be of variable size, but they must occur at regular intervals. The interval should be the same as the period of the discount rate.

MFPF puts 10% of profits each month for the year 2000 in a bank account with a negligible interest rate. Inflation for the year was 5.5%, or approximately 0.46% per month.

The total amount of money saved over the year was £2089.65. Taking inflation into account, what would the NPV of MFPF's £2089.65 savings have been at the start of the 12-month period?

In the next exercise, you will calculate the NPV of MFPF's savings at the start of the investment period.

Exercise 14.1: Using NPV

1) Open MFPF_FINANCE.XLS and go to the *PROFIT* worksheet.

2) In cell *H1*, enter the label *Savings*.

3) In cell *H2*, enter the formula = _D2*0.1, to calculate 10% of the profit value in column *D*.
    The ' _ ' is because the amounts are then paid into a savings account.
    Copy the formula to the other cells in the range *H2:H13*.

4) In cell *A18*, enter the label *Discount Rate*.

5) In cell *B18*, enter the formula =0.055/12 to calculate the monthly rate of inflation.

6) In cell *A19*, enter the label *NPV*.

7) In cell *B19*, enter the formula =*NPV(B18,H2:H13)*.
The result tells you that the NPV of the investment at the start of the year was £2034.93.

MFPF can buy £2089.65 worth of goods at the end of the year, using the money saved. Twelve months earlier, the same goods would have cost £2034.93. Prices will have increased due to the 5.5% annual inflation rate.

PV

PV is an Excel function, similar to NPV, that calculates the present value of an investment where all the payments made are the same size and made at regular intervals.

The financial function PV has the following format:

=PV(Rate, Nper, Pmt, Fv, Type)	
Rate	The discount rate per period.
Nper	The number of payment periods in the investment.
Pmt	The value of the payment made each period. This value cannot change over the lifetime of the investment. **Note:** You must supply a value for either *Pmt* or *Fv*, but not both.
Fv	The future value the investment or debt should reach at maturity. If you are paying back a loan, the value of *Fv* is *0*. If you do not fill in a value, *0* is assumed. **Note:** You must supply a value for either *Pmt* or *Fv*, but not both.
Type	*1* or *0*. *1* indicates that payment is made at the start of each period, and *0* that it is made at the end of the period. If you do not specify a value, *0* is assumed.

If MFPF had invested £150 each month instead of 10% of profits, £1800 would have been saved over the year. What would the PV of the £1800 have been at the start of the 12-month period?

In the next exercise, you will calculate the PV at the start of the investment period of £150 savings per month over the 12-month period.

Exercise 14.2: Using PV

1) Open MFPF_FINANCE.XLS and go to the *PROFIT* worksheet.

2) In cell *A20*, enter the label *Fixed sum*.

3) In cell *B20*, enter the value *−150*.

4) In cell *A21*, enter the label *PV*.

5) In cell *B21*, enter the formula *=PV(B18,12,B20)*.
   Cell *B18* contains the *Rate value*, 12 is the number of payment periods (*Nper*), and cell *B20* contains the value for *Pmt*. No values are specified for the *Fv* or *Type* parameters.
   The result tells you that the PV of the investment at the start of the year was £1747.50.

FV

FV is an Excel function used to calculate the future value of an investment or debt, where fixed payments are made at regular intervals. FV only considers the interest rate being applied to the investment or debt, and ignores inflation and devaluation.

The financial function FV has the following format:

=FV(Rate, Nper, Pmt, Pv, Type)	
Rate	The interest rate per period.
Nper	The number of payment periods in the investment.
Pmt	The value of the payment made each period. This value cannot change over the lifetime of the investment. **Note:** You must supply a value for either *Pmt* or *Pv*, but not both.
Pv	The present value of all of the future payments. If you do not fill in a value, *0* is assumed. **Note:** You must supply a value for either *Pmt* or *Pv*, but not both.
Type	*1* or *0*. *1* indicates that payment is made at the start of each period, and *0* that it is made at the end of the period. If you do not specify a value, *0* is assumed.

The Murphys are considering opening a savings account that will pay 7.5% interest per annum if at least £200 is deposited each month. If MFPF invests £200 each month for 12 months, how much money will there be in the account, including interest?

In the next exercise, you will calculate how much money will be in the savings account at the end of a year if £200 is invested monthly.

Exercise 14.3: Using FV

1) Open MFPF_FINANCE.XLS and go to the *PROFIT* worksheet.

2) In cell *A23*, enter the label *Fixed sum*.

3) In cell *B23*, enter the value *–200*.

4) In cell *A24*, enter the label *Interest rate*.

5) In cell *B24*, enter the formula *=0.075/12*.

6) In cell *A25*, enter the label *FV*.

7) In cell *B25*, enter the formula *=FV(B24, 12, B23)*.
    Cell *B24* contains the *Rate value*, 12 is the number of payment periods, and cell *B23* contains the value for *Pmt*.
    The result tells you that the future value of an account where £200 is invested each month for 12 months at an annual interest rate of 7.5% is £2484.24.

PMT

You can use Excel's PMT function to calculate the size of fixed payments needed on an investment or debt in order to reach a target value in a certain number of payments, where you already know the interest rate per period.

The financial function PMT has the following format:

=PMT(Rate, Nper, Pv, Fv, Type)	
Rate	The interest rate per period.
Nper	The number of payment periods in the investment.
Pv	The present value of all of the future payments combined. If you are calculating the size of payments to pay back a loan, this is the value of the loan. If you do not fill in a value, *0* is assumed.
Fv	The future value the investment or debt should reach at maturity. If you are paying back a loan, the value of *Fv* is *0*. If you do not fill in a value, *0* is assumed.
Type	*1* or *0*. *1* indicates that payment is made at the start of each period, and *0* that it is made at the end of the period. If you do not specify a value, *0* is assumed.

Mr Murphy would like to buy a new delivery van. A local showroom has promised to sell him one used for display and test drives for £5500 at the end of next year. MFPF already has £2089.65 in savings from last year, so the company needs to save a further £3410.35 in the next 12 months to be able to buy the van.

Mr Murphy asks you to work out how much he would need to save each month in the account offering 7.5% interest per annum if he wanted to save exactly £3410.35 after 12 months, including interest.

In the next exercise, you will calculate the payment Mr Murphy must make into the savings account to achieve his target in 12 months.

Exercise 14.4: Using PMT

1) Open MFPF_FINANCE.XLS and go to the *PROFIT* worksheet.

2) In cell *A26*, enter the label *PMT*.

3) In cell *B26*, enter the formula =*PMT(B24, 12, 0, 3410.35)*.
   Cell *B24* contains the interest rate, 12 is the number of payment periods, 0 is the present value of the account, and £3410.35 is the target final value.

Chapter 14: Using Financial Functions

The result tells you that MFPF needs to put £274.56 in the savings account each month to save £3410.35, including interest, by the end of the 12-month period.

RATE

RATE is an Excel financial function used to determine the interest rate on an investment where the number of payments and constant payment size are known, as well as either the PV or FV of the investment.

The financial function RATE has the following format:

=RATE(Nper, Pmt, Pv, Fv, Type, Guess)	
Nper	The number of payment periods in the investment.
Pmt	The value of the payment made each period. This value cannot change over the lifetime of the investment. **Note:** If you do not supply a value for *Pmt*, you must supply one for *Fv*.
Pv	The present value of all of the future payments combined. If you are calculating the size of payments to pay back a loan, this is the value of the loan. If you do not fill in a value, *0* is assumed.
Fv	The future value the investment or debt should reach at maturity. If you are paying back a loan, the value of *Fv* is *0*. If you do not fill in a value, *0* is assumed. **Note:** If you do not supply a value for *Fv*, you must supply one for *Pmt*.
Type	*1* or *0*. *1* indicates that payment is made at the start of each period, and *0* that it is made at the end of the period. If you do not specify a value, *0* is assumed.
Guess	Your guess for what you think the rate will be. This field can be left blank. If you do not supply a guess, 10% is assumed.

Mr Murphy has asked you to find out what interest rate an account should have for him to be able to save enough to pay for the new van by investing only £265 per month.

In the next exercise, you will work out the optimum interest rate for a savings account, so that the final amount in the account after 12 months will be £3410.35, including interest, when £265 is invested each month.

Exercise 14.5: Using RATE

1) Open MFPF_FINANCE.XLS and go to the *PROFIT* worksheet.

2) In cell *A28*, enter the label *Rate*.

3) In cell *B28*, enter the formula *=RATE(12, –265, 0, 3410.35)*.
   The result tells you that Mr Murphy will need to find a savings account offering 1.26% interest per month (equivalent to 15.15% per annum) to achieve his target in 12 months.
   (You may need to apply cell formatting to see this result to two decimal places.)

Chapter summary

Excel's NPV function calculates the net present value of an investment or debt, where payments are at regular intervals but of variable size. PV is similar to NPV, but calculates the present value of an investment where all the payments are the same size and made at regular intervals.

FV calculates the future value of an investment or debt, where fixed payments are made at regular intervals.

PMT calculates the size of fixed payments needed on an investment or debt in order to reach a target value in a certain number of payments, where you already know the interest rate per period.

RATE determines the interest rate on an investment where the number of payments and constant payment size are known as well as either the PV or FV of the investment.

15

Using Text and Date Functions

In this chapter

In general, you will use Excel spreadsheets to keep track of numeric information and to perform numeric calculations. But there are other types of data you can include in your spreadsheets – for example, text and dates.

Excel includes a number of functions that you can use to manipulate text and date information in your spreadsheets.

In this chapter you will learn how to manipulate text data, change the case, and create concatenated strings.

You will also learn about the date functions in Excel, which allow you to generate and manipulate date information.

New skills

At the end of this chapter you should be able to:

- Use the PROPER, UPPER and LOWER text functions
- Use the CONCATENATE text function
- Use the TODAY date function
- Use the DAY, MONTH and YEAR date functions

New words

At the end of this chapter you should be able to explain the following term:

- String

Text functions

Earlier, you looked at functions, such as ROUND, that took numeric values as arguments, made some change to the value, and displayed the result. There are also Excel functions that take text values as arguments, make a change to the text, and display the result.

In this chapter, you will learn about text functions that allow you to change the case (upper or lower) of text, and that allow you to combine text values into longer strings, and to combine text and numeric values into a single value.

String
A string is a value that contains text, or text and numbers.

Note: When using a string as an argument to a function in Excel, you must enclose it in double quotation marks (").

PROPER

PROPER is an Excel function that takes a string as an argument and capitalizes the first letter of each word.

In the next exercise, you will add a formula to a cell in PASTE_SPECIAL.XLS that retrieves the string in another cell, reformats it with the first letter of each word capitalized, and displays the result.

Exercise 15.1: Using PROPER

1) Open PASTE_SPECIAL.XLS. Note that cell *A12* contains the string "y0uR vAlUe HeRe".

2) In cell *A28*, enter the formula =*PROPER(A12)*.
   The text from cell *A12* is now shown in cell *A28*, reformatted so that the first letter of each word is capitalized.

UPPER

UPPER is an Excel function that takes a string as an argument and capitalizes every letter.

In the next exercise, you will add a formula to another cell in PASTE_SPECIAL.XLS that will retrieve the PROPER case string you generated in *Exercise 15.1* and reformat it with every letter capitalized.

Exercise 15.2: Using UPPER

1) Open PASTE_SPECIAL.XLS.

2) In cell *A29*, enter the formula =*UPPER(A28)*.
   The text from cell *A28* is shown in cell *A29*, reformatted so that every letter is capitalized.

LOWER

LOWER is an Excel function that takes a string as an argument and changes every letter to lower case.

In the next exercise, you will add a formula to another cell in PASTE_SPECIAL.XLS, retrieve the upper-case string you generated in *Exercise 15.2*, and reformat it with every letter in lower case.

Exercise 15.3: Using LOWER

1) Open PASTE_SPECIAL.XLS.

2) In cell *A30*, enter the formula =*LOWER(A29)*.
   The text from cell *A29* is shown in cell *A30*, reformatted so that every letter is in lower case.

Reusing text values in longer strings

Sometimes, you may want to join values together in a spreadsheet to create new strings. For example, say a spreadsheet listing staff members has first names in column *A* and surnames in column *B*. You could join the values from the cells in columns *A* and *B* in each row together to generate full names.

Joining a series of text strings together is known as concatenation, and Excel has a text function, CONCATENATE, that can do just that.

CONCATENATE

CONCATENATE is an Excel function that takes a series of arguments separated by commas and joins them together to create a single string. Arguments can be cell references, numbers or text.

Note: When using CONCATENATE, you must include any spaces you want to appear between concatenated terms. The spaces should appear inside quotation marks or they will be ignored. Space is not added automatically between arguments.

In the next exercise, you will use the CONCATENATE function to join two strings and the value from a cell together to create a new string.

Exercise 15.4: Using CONCATENATE

1) Open PASTE_SPECIAL.XLS.

2) In cell *A32*, enter the formula =*CONCATENATE("The text in cell A12 says: ",A12,"!!")* and press **ENTER**.
    The value in cell A32 is now: *The text in cell A12 says: yOuR vAlUe HeRe:!!*

3) Save and close your workbook when you are done.

Date

Excel's date functions allow you to generate and manipulate date information. In this section, you will look at formulae that allow you to automatically retrieve the current day's date, and to display individual elements of a date, such as the month.

TODAY

TODAY is an Excel date function that returns the current date. This function can be a useful timesaver, as you neither have to find the current date nor type it in.

In the next exercise, you will edit the invoice template, INVOICE_MFPF.XLT, and add the TODAY function to automatically fill in the date when an invoice is edited.

> **Note:** When you have finished writing an invoice, you should use **Copy** and **Paste Special** to replace the date formula with the value it generates. Otherwise, the next time you open the document to read or edit it, the date will be updated again.

Exercise 15.5: Using TODAY

1) Create a new spreadsheet based on the INVOICE_MFPF.XLT template.

2) In cell *F5*, enter the formula *=TODAY()*.

3) Save the spreadsheet as a template, replacing the original INVOICE_MFPF.XLT.

DAY, MONTH and YEAR

DAY, MONTH, and YEAR are Excel functions that take a date as an argument, and return the number value of the day, month and year portions of that date, respectively.

In the next exercise, you will use CONCATENATE in conjunction with DAY, MONTH and YEAR to create a sentence that lists the number values for the day, month and year of the date generated by TODAY.

Exercise 15.6: Using DAY, MONTH and YEAR

1) Open a new, blank spreadsheet.

2) In cell *A1*, enter the label *Today's date*.

3) In cell *A2*, enter the formula *=TODAY()*.
   In cell *C1*, enter the formula *=CONCATENATE("Today is day ",DAY(A2)," of month ",MONTH(A2),", ",YEAR(A2),".")*

4) Close the workbook without saving when finished.

Chapter summary

A string is a value that contains text, or text and numbers.

The PROPER text function takes a string as an argument and capitalizes the first letter of each word. UPPER capitalizes every letter, and LOWER reformats the text so that every letter is in lower case.

CONCATENATE takes a series of strings and joins them all together to create a single string. Arguments can be cell references, numbers or text.

The TODAY date function returns the current date. The DAY, MONTH and YEAR functions take a date as an argument and return the number value of the day, month and year portions of that date, respectively.

16 Using Logical Functions

In this chapter

Earlier, you learned how to apply formatting to a cell if the value it contained satisfied certain criteria (conditional formatting). Sometimes, you may want to check whether a value satisfies certain criteria but not do anything to the data itself.

For example, you might want to check if your profits for any month are below a certain value, but not apply any special formatting to the value. Otherwise it will be the first thing a bank manager or prospective investor notices when looking at your accounts!

Excel's logical functions allow you to check the value of data in a cell against certain criteria. The functions return a value of TRUE if the criteria are satisfied, and FALSE if they are not.

New skills

At the end of this chapter you should be able to:

- Use the IF function
- Use the AND and OR functions
- Use the ISERROR function

New words

There are no new words in this chapter.

IF

Excel's logical functions are used to check if the value in a cell satisfies certain criteria. They return a value of *TRUE* if it does, and *FALSE* if it does not.

You can use Excel's IF function to perform a logical test and return custom messages for *TRUE* and *FALSE* results. The logical test can be any comparison using the operators <, >, =, <= (which means less than or equal to) or >= (which means greater than or equal to), and can include cell references as well as numeric and text values. The logical test can even be another logical function – for example, an AND test.

The logical function IF has the following format:

=IF(Logical_test, Value_if_true, Value_if_false)	
Logical_test	The logical test or comparison to perform, for example, *A1>B1*.
Value_if_true	The value to return if the result of the logical test is *TRUE*. If the value is a string, it should be enclosed in quotation marks – for example, *"Passed Test"*.
Value_if_false	The value to return if the result of the logical test is *FALSE*. If the value is a string, it should be enclosed in quotation marks – for example, *"Failed Test"*.

Mrs Murphy has asked you to indicate, beside the profit figure for each month, whether the profits have gone up or down from the previous month.

In the next exercise, you will use the IF function to compare the profit figure for each month with the one for the previous month. You will return a message of *UP* if a month's profit is greater than the profit for the previous month, and *DOWN* if it is less than the profit for the previous month.

Exercise 16.1: Using IF

1) Open MFPF_FINANCE.XLS and go to the *PROFIT* worksheet.

2) Select column *F*, where you calculated rounded profit using a single formula, and delete its contents.

3) In cell *F1*, enter the label *TREND*.

4) In cell *F3*, enter the formula =*IF(D3>D2,"UP","DOWN")*.

5) Copy the formula to the other cells in the range *F3:F13*.
As you do not have a profit value for December 1999 to compare with the January 2000 value, you should not enter a formula in cell *F2*.

6) Save your workbook when you are done.

Over to you: mandatory

In the invoice template, **INVOICE_MFPF.XLT**, the white text *Late* in cell *D9* is conditionally formatted in red if the customer pays more than 28 days after the invoice was issued. If you changed the fill colour of cell *D9* to any other colour, the white text would be visible. Use the IF function to generate the *Late* text instead.

- Create a new spreadsheet based on the template **INVOICE_MFPF.XLT**.

- Delete the text in cell *D9* on the **PERSONAL NOTES** worksheet, and change the text colour for the cell to black.

- Add an IF function to the cell, which checks whether the difference between *Date Paid* and *Date Invoiced* is greater than 28, and returns the text *Late* if it is, and no message otherwise.

- Save the spreadsheet as a template, replacing the original **INVOICE_MFPF.XLT**.

AND

AND is an Excel function that examines a list of logical tests or comparisons, and returns a value of *TRUE* if *all* of the logical tests are true. Otherwise, the function returns a value of *FALSE*.

The logical function AND has the following format:

=AND(Logical1, Logical2, ...)	
Logical1, Logical2, ...	The list of logical tests or comparisons to perform.

To return a custom message instead of TRUE or FALSE, you could nest this function in an IF function, as the *Logical_test* argument.

For example, the formula
=IF(AND(B1<2,B2<2),"Both < 2","Not both < 2")
returns the string *Both < 2* if the values in both cells *B1* and *B2*
are less than 2, making the AND function return *TRUE*, and
returns the string *Not both < 2* if the AND function returns
FALSE.

Mr Murphy is wondering whether he should sell garden tables
and garden chairs packaged together as sets. He asks you to look
at the orders for the last year to see if customers usually buy
both garden chairs and garden tables at the same time.

In the next exercise, you will use the logical AND function to
find the orders where both garden chairs and garden tables were
ordered at the same time.

Exercise 16.2: Using AND

1) Open MFPF_ORD.XLS and go to the *COMPLETE* worksheet.

2) In cell *K1*, enter the label *Chairs and Tables*.

3) In cell *K2*, enter the formula =AND(I2>0,J2>0).

4) Copy the formula to the other cells in column *K*.
   The message *TRUE* appears in the rows where both garden chairs and
   garden tables were ordered.
   The message *FALSE* appears where either no garden chairs or garden
   tables were ordered, or where only one or the other was ordered.

OR

OR is an Excel function that examines a list of logical tests or
comparisons, and returns a value of *TRUE* if one or more of the
logical tests is true. Otherwise, the function returns a value of
FALSE.

The logical function OR has the following format:

=OR(Logical1, Logical2, ...)	
Logical1, Logical2, ...	The list of logical tests or comparisons to perform.

The results in column *K* show which customers bought both garden tables and garden chairs. Next, you will see who bought garden tables or garden chairs or both, using the OR function. By comparing the values, you will be able to see who bought one but not the other.

In the next exercise, you will use the OR function to check which customers ordered either garden chairs or garden tables or both.

Exercise 16.3: Using OR

1) Open MFPF_ORD.XLS and go to the *COMPLETE* worksheet.

2) In cell *L1*, enter the label *Chair and/or Tables*.

3) In cell *L2*, enter the formula *=OR(I2>0,J2>0)*.

4) Copy the formula to the other cells in column *L*.
   Orders where either garden chairs or garden tables were ordered, and orders where both garden chairs and garden tables were ordered, are now flagged as *TRUE* in column *L*.

Over to you: mandatory

By looking at columns *K* and *L* together, you can see which customers bought either garden chairs or garden tables but not both of them. You could see this information more clearly if you used another logical function to compare the results of both tests.

- In column *M*, use an AND function to flag orders that have a *FALSE* value in column *K* and a *TRUE* value in column *L*. A *TRUE* result in column *M* indicates an order where either chairs or tables but not both were bought.

Over to you: optional

You could also construct a nested function to perform this check in a single step.

- Create an AND function that uses AND and OR functions as arguments to determine which customers bought either garden chairs or garden tables, but not both.

ISERROR

ISERROR is an Excel function that examines the value in a cell, and returns a value of *TRUE* if the value is an Excel error message. Otherwise, the function returns a value of *FALSE*.

The information function ISERROR has the following format:

=ISERROR(Value)	
Value	The cell to check for an error message.

You have decided to add a worksheet to MFPF_FINANCE.XLS that will contain ISERROR checks for all of the formulae used in the workbook. This means that when you make changes to the data in your workbook, you can see quickly and easily if your changes contravene any of the formulae you use just by looking at this one sheet.

In the next exercise, you will add a new worksheet to MFPF_FINANCE.XLS and start adding ISERROR checks for cells containing formulae.

Exercise 16.4: Using ISERROR

1) Open MFPF_FINANCE.XLS and add a new worksheet.
   Name the new worksheet *ERRORS*.

2) In cell *A1*, enter the label *NPV.*

3) In cell *B1*, enter the formula *=ISERROR(PROFIT!B19)*.
   The value is *FALSE* because there is no error in cell *B19* on the *PROFIT* worksheet.

Over to you: optional

If you would like to reassure yourself that the ISERROR function really works, go to the *PROFIT* worksheet and edit the NPV formula to say *=NPV(I2,E2:E13)/0*. This generates a *#DIV/0!* error, and changes the value in cell *B1* on the *ERRORS* worksheet to *TRUE*.

Chapter summary

Excel's logical functions are used to check if the value in a cell satisfies certain criteria. They return a value of *TRUE* if it does, and *FALSE* if it does not.

IF performs a logical test and can return custom messages for *TRUE* and *FALSE* results.

AND examines a list of logical tests or comparisons, and returns a value of *TRUE* if *all* of the logical tests are true. OR returns a value of *TRUE* if one or more of the logical tests is true.

ISERROR examines the value in a cell, and returns a value of *TRUE* if the value is an Excel error message.

17

Using Data Tables and Scenarios

What if you invested in a savings account with a 4% interest rate instead of one with a 3% interest rate? What if you invested £170 per month instead of £150? What effect would one or more of these changes have on the value of your savings in a year's time?

To answer questions like these, where you have several alternative values you could use for an argument and you want to know what the result would be if you used each of them, you could create a formula for each possibility and enter it in your spreadsheet.

Aside from this method, Excel offers you two ways to deal with such 'What if?' calculations: data tables and scenarios.

In this chapter you will learn how to use each of these tools.

New skills

At the end of this chapter you should be able to:

- Use a 1-input data table
- Use a 2-input data table
- Create a named scenario
- View a named scenario
- Generate a scenario summary report

New words

At the end of this chapter you should be able to explain the following terms:

- Data table
- Scenario

Data tables

In Chapter 14, you calculated how much money Mr Murphy needed to save each month in an account with a particular interest rate to have saved a target amount at the end of 12 months. Then you calculated what interest rate an account would need to attract for him to be able to save a smaller amount each month and reach the same goal.

You could have created a data table to find the ideal combination of RATE and PMT values to achieve a target FV result.

Data table
A data table is a range of cells that shows the results of substituting different values in one or more formulae.

There are two types of data table:

- *1-input data table*: In a 1-input data table, you can substitute different values for one variable, and see the effect each value has on the results of one or more formulae.
- *2-input data table*: In a 2-input data table, you can substitute different values for two variables, and see the effect each variable value combination has on a single formula.

1-input data tables

With a 1-input data table, you can see the effect that changing a single variable value has on the results of any number of formulae that use that value. You could have used a 1-input data table to work out the future value your savings would have for a range of different interest rates.

A 1-input data table lists the possible values for a single variable on one axis and a series of formulae that use that value on the other axis. Excel completes the data table by filling in the results for each of the formulae using the different variable values.

In the following example, a 1-input data table has been set up with a list of possible interest rates in a column orientation and an FV formula in a row orientation. Results have not yet been calculated.

The FV formula will be used to calculate the possible future values of an investment of a fixed sum of £200 over 12 payment periods. Initially, the FV formula takes the interest rate value from cell *B1*. To fill in the data table with the value of FV for each interest rate, you must tell Excel to replace the value in cell *B1* with the values in the column axis of the table.

	A	B	C	D
1	Interest rate per period	0.0025		
2				
3			=FV(B1,12,-200)	
4		0.0025		
5		0.005		
6		0.0075		
7		0.01		
8		0.0125		
9		0.015		
10				

(Column A, rows 4–9 labelled vertically: *Interest rates*)

The formulae refer to a specific cell on the worksheet, but the value in that cell is replaced by each variable value to calculate the final results.

> **Note:** If you enter your variables in a *column* orientation, you should add your first formula in the cell one column to the right of, and one row above, the cell containing the first variable value. Any other formulae should be entered in the cells to the right of the first formula.
>
> If you enter your variable in a *row* orientation, you should add your first formula in the cell one column to the left of, and one row below, the cell containing the first variable value. Any other formulae should be entered in the cells below the first formula.

In the next exercise, you will create the 1-input data table shown in the example, and fill in the final results.

Exercise 17.1: Using a 1-input data table

1) Create a new worksheet, based on the default template, and save it as INVEST.XLS.

2) In cell *A1* of the first worksheet, enter the label *Interest rate per period*.

3) In cell *B1*, enter the value *0.0025* – a quarter of one per cent.

4) In cell *A4*, enter the label *Interest Rates*.

5) Change the formatting of cell *A4* so that the text in it is bold and rotated through 90 degrees.

6) In the cell range *B4:B9*, enter the variable values *0.0025*, *0.005*, *0.0075*, *0.01*, *0.0125* and *0.015*.
These are the variable values you will substitute in place of the interest rate in cell *B1*.

7) In cell *C3*, enter the formula *=FV(B1,12,_200)*.

8) Select the range *B3:C9*, and select **Data | Table ...** .
The *Table* dialog box opens.

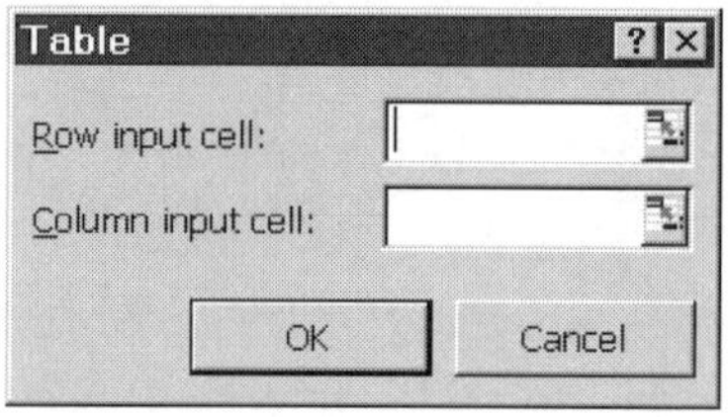

9) In this dialog box, you will tell Excel which cell referred to in your formulae should be replaced by the variable values in either the column or row orientation in your data table.
Enter the cell *B1* in the *Column input cell* field.
Click **OK**.
The data table is filled in with the values calculated for FV with each possible interest rate.

	A	B	C	D
1	**Interest rate per period**	0.0025		
2				
3			2433.276553	
4	**Interest rates**	0.0025	2433.276553	
5		0.005	2467.112475	
6		0.0075	2501.517271	
7		0.01	2536.500603	
8		0.0125	2572.072284	
9		0.015	2608.242286	
10				

(You may need to apply additional cell formatting to see your results to the same number of decimal places shown in the illustration.)

10) Save your workbook when you are done.

2-input data tables

You can also create a 2-input data table to calculate the possible results of a single formula where the values of two of the inputs can change. For example, to calculate FV, if there are a variety of interest rates to choose from, and several possible values for PMT, you could create a 2-input data table.

In this case, one set of variables is entered in the row orientation of the data table and the other in the column orientation.

The formula should be entered in the cell immediately above the first entry in the column of variable values, and the row of variable values should be entered in the cell range starting with the first cell to the right of the formula.

In the next exercise, you will create a 2-input data table that calculates the value of FV where both the interest rate per period and the payment amount are variables.

Exercise 17.2: Using a 2-input data table

1) In cell *C1* of the first worksheet in INVEST.XLS, enter the label *Payment*.

2) In cell *D1*, enter the value *–150*.

3) In cell *A11*, enter the formula *=FV(B1,12,D1)*.
   Cell *B1* contains the value for *Rate*, 12 is the number of payment periods, and cell *D1* contains the value for *Pmt* (the payment amount).

4) In the cell range *A12:A17*, enter the variable values *0.0025*, *0.005*, *0.0075*, *0.01*, *0.0125* and *0.015*.
   These are the variable values you will substitute for the interest rate in cell *B1*.

5) In the cell range *B11:G11*, enter the variable values *–150*, *–160*, *–170*, *–180*, *–190* and *–200*.
   These are the variable values you will substitute for the payment amount in cell *D1*.

6) Select the cell range *A11:G17* and select **Data | Table** ... .
   The *Table* dialog box opens.

7) In the *Column Input Cell* field, enter *B1*.
   In the *Row Input Cell* field, enter *D1*.
   Click **OK**.

The data table is filled in with the values calculated for FV with each interest rate and payment amount combination.

	A	B	C	D	E	F	G
1	Interest rate per period	0.0025	Payment	-150			
2							
3			$2,433.28				
4	Interest Rates	0.0025	2433.277				
5		0.005	2467.112				
6		0.0075	2501.517				
7		0.01	2536.501				
8		0.0125	2572.072				
9		0.015	2608.242				
10							
11	1824.9574	-150	-160	-170	-180	-190	-200
12	0.0025	1824.957	1946.621	2068.285	2189.949	2311.613	2433.277
13	0.005	1850.334	1973.69	2097.046	2220.401	2343.757	2467.112
14	0.0075	1876.138	2001.214	2126.29	2251.366	2376.441	2501.517
15	0.01	1902.375	2029.2	2156.026	2282.851	2409.676	2536.501
16	0.0125	1929.054	2057.658	2186.261	2314.865	2443.469	2572.072
17	0.015	1956.182	2086.594	2217.006	2347.418	2477.83	2608.242
18							

8) Save your workbook when you are done.

Named scenarios

What if you wanted to substitute a variable number of payment periods in the formula, too? You cannot do this in a data table, but you can use Excel's Scenarios functionality to substitute values for any number of variables.

> **Scenario**
>
> *A scenario is a named set of values that can be substituted into a set of selected cells in a spreadsheet.*

When you create a scenario, you define a set of values that should be entered in particular cells on a worksheet, and assign a name to that scenario. You can select any one scenario to view at one time, and all the defined values in that scenario are substituted into your worksheet.

Creating a scenario

In the next exercise, you will create a scenario that specifies a particular combination of values for the number of payment periods in an investment, the payment amount per period, and the interest rate per period.

Exercise 17.3: Creating a named scenario

1) In cell *E1* of the first worksheet in INVEST.XLS, enter the label *Payment Periods*.

2) In cell *F1*, enter the value *12*.

3) In cell *A2*, enter the label *FV*.

4) In cell *B2*, enter the formula *=FV(B1,F1,D1)*.
Cell *B1* contains the value for *Rate*, cell *F1* contains the value for *Nper* (the number of payment periods), and cell *D1* contains the value for *Pmt*.

5) Select **Tools | Scenarios ...** .
The *Scenario Manager* dialog box opens.

6) Click **Add ...** .
The *Add Scenario* dialog box opens.

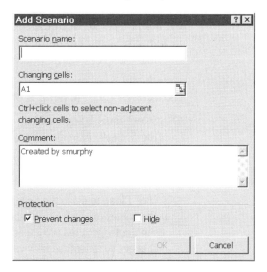

7) In the *Scenario name* field, enter *Savings1*.
In the *Changing cells* field, enter *B1,D1,F1*.
Click **OK**.
The *Scenario Values* dialog box opens.

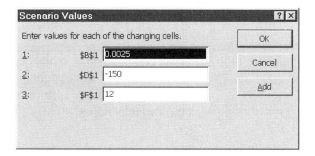

8) In the *Scenario Values* dialog box, the current values in the selected cells are shown.
You can edit one or more of these values, and save all three in the current scenario by clicking **OK**.
For now, you will save the default values in the *Savings1* scenario.

9) Click **OK**.

10) Click **Close** to close the *Scenario Manager* dialog box.

Over to you: mandatory

Continue to add scenarios using different combinations of values for interest rate per period in cell *B1*, number of periods in the investment in cell *F1*, and payment amount per period in cell *D1*. Add at least two more scenarios.

Viewing a scenario

When you have defined your scenarios, you can select any one of them to view. All of the scenario values you defined are filled in to the selected changing cells, and the results of any formulae that use these cells are updated.

Exercise 17.4: Viewing a scenario

1) Select **Tools | Scenarios ...** .
The *Scenario Manager* dialog box opens.

2) In the *Scenarios* area, select one of the two additional scenarios you defined and click **Show**.

3) Click **Close** to close the *Scenario Manager* dialog box.
The values for cells *B1*, *D1* and *F1* specified in the scenario are substituted into the worksheet and the result of the formula in cell *B2* changes to reflect the new values in cells *B1*, *D1* and *F1*.

4) Save your workbook when you are done.

Scenario summaries

Unlike data tables, which show all possible results at once, you can only see the data for one scenario at a time. This makes it difficult to compare the effect each set of values has just by looking at the results.

Excel allows you to create scenario summary reports, which show the set of values defined in each scenario and also the final numbers in selected results cells on the worksheet that rely on the variable values.

In the next exercise, you will create a summary report that shows the settings for, and results of, each scenario you have defined on the first worksheet of INVEST.XLS.

Exercise 17.5: Creating a scenario summary

1) Select **Tools | Scenarios** ... .

2) Click **Summary** ... .
   The *Scenario Summary* dialog box opens.

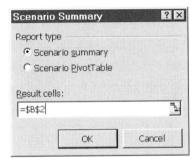

3) In the *Report type* area, select *Scenario summary*.

4) In the *Result cells* area, enter *$B$2*.
   This is the cell that contains the FV formula that uses the data from the changing cells.

5) Click **OK**.

6) A new worksheet is added to your workbook.
   The worksheet contains a summary report of the scenarios you defined. It shows the changing cells and their values for each scenario, as well as the results cells and their values.

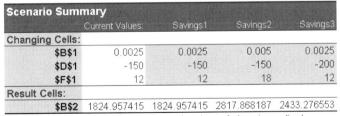

Scenario Summary				
	Current Values:	Savings1	Savings2	Savings3
Changing Cells:				
$B$1	0.0025	0.0025	0.005	0.0025
$D$1	-150	-150	-150	-200
$F$1	12	12	18	12
Result Cells:				
$B$2	1824.957415	1824.957415	2817.868187	2433.276553

Notes: Current Values column represents values of changing cells at time Scenario Summary Report was created. Changing cells for each scenario are highlighted in gray.

7) Save and close your workbook when you are done.

Chapter summary

A data table is a range of cells that shows the results of substituting different values in one or more formulae.

There are two types of data table:

- *1-input data table*: In a 1-input data table, you can substitute different values for one variable, and see the effect each value has on the results of one or more formulae.
- *2-input data table*: In a 2-input data table, you can substitute different values for two variables, and see the effect each variable value combination has on a single formula.

A scenario is a named set of values that can be substituted into a set of selected cells in a spreadsheet. You can only view one scenario at a time.

You can create scenario summary reports that show the set of values defined in each scenario and also the final numbers in selected results cells on the worksheet that rely on the variable values.

18

Auditing your Spreadsheets

In this chapter

Congratulations! Your workbooks are now completed. You have entered or imported all of the required data, and you have made all of your calculations.

But how can you tell which cells contain pure values, and which contain formulae? How can you track which formulae use data from which cells?

In this chapter, you will learn how to audit your worksheets to locate the cells containing formulae, and to track which cells contain values used in formulae, and which cells contain the formulae that use them.

New skills

At the end of this chapter you should be able to:

- Locate and display formulae on a worksheet
- Trace precedent and dependent cells

New words

There are no new words in this chapter.

Formulae and locations

In *Exercise 16.4* on page 144, you started to add ISERROR functions to a worksheet, which would check the formulae in your workbook for errors. But, how can you tell which cells in your worksheets contain formulae, without checking each cell individually?

Excel allows you to identify the cells in a worksheet that contain formulae in two ways:

- Using the **Go To** command to select all the cells that contain formulae.

- Choosing to display the formulae in cells, instead of the values they generate.

Go To

In the next exercise, you will use Excel's **Go To** command to select all of the cells on the *PROFIT* worksheet of MFPF_FINANCE.XLS that contain formulae.

Exercise 18.1: Highlighting cells that contain formulae

1) Open MFPF_FINANCE.XLS and go to the *PROFIT* worksheet.

2) Select **Edit | Go To ...** .
   The *Go To* dialog box opens.
   This dialog box lists named cell ranges on the current worksheet.
   If you select a range and click **OK**, that range is selected in the worksheet.

3) Click **Special ...** .
The *Go To Special* dialog box opens.

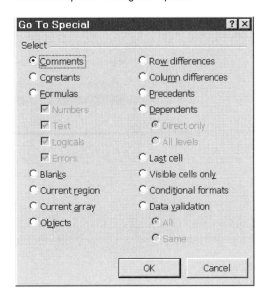

This dialog box lets you select a particular cell property that the cells you want to select have.
When you click **OK**, any cell with the selected property is selected. If multiple cells have the property, they are all selected.

4) Select *Formulas*, and check all of the formula types.

5) Click **OK**.
All of the cells on the *PROFIT* worksheet that contain formulae are now selected.

You can select all cells containing formulae using **Go To**, but to see the actual formula in a given cell, you need to select that cell and read the formula from the formula bar. When you do this, you deselect all of the other cells again.

Displaying formulae

You can specify that you want to show all formulae in a worksheet instead of the values they generate.

In the next exercise, you will display all of the formulae in the *INCOMING* worksheet of MFPF_FINANCE.XLS.

Exercise 18.2: Showing formulae instead of values

1) Go to the *INCOMING* worksheet of MFPF_FINANCE.XLS.

2) Press **Ctrl** and ' (the open single inverted comma key).
The formulae used to calculate values on this sheet are shown instead of the values.

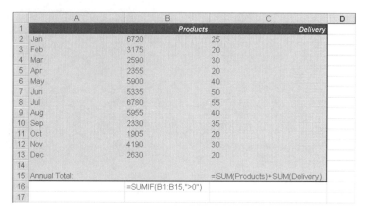

	A	B	C	D
1		*Products*	*Delivery*	
2	Jan	6720	25	
3	Feb	3175	20	
4	Mar	2590	30	
5	Apr	2355	20	
6	May	5900	40	
7	Jun	5335	50	
8	Jul	6780	55	
9	Aug	5955	40	
10	Sep	2330	35	
11	Oct	1905	20	
12	Nov	4190	30	
13	Dec	2630	20	
14				
15	Annual Total:		=SUM(Products)+SUM(Delivery)	
16		=SUMIF(B1:B15,">0")		
17				

You can toggle between formulae and values by pressing **Ctrl** and ' repeatedly.

Tracing precedent cells

Without reading the list of arguments for a formula, how can you tell which cells it gets data from?

Excel's **Trace Precedents** command locates all of the cells referred to by the formula in a selected cell, and connects them to the cell containing the formula using arrows.

If any of the precedent cells are not on the same worksheet as the selected cell, a spreadsheet icon is shown at the other end of the precedent's arrow.

If you double-click the spreadsheet icon, the *Go To* dialog box opens with a list of all the precedent cells not on the current worksheet. You can select one of these cell references and click **OK** to go to that cell.

In the next exercise, you will use the **Trace Precedents** command to indicate the cells that contain input data for the NPV formula on the *PROFIT* worksheet of MFPF_FINANCE.XLS.

Exercise 18.3: Tracing precedent cells

1) Open MFPF_FINANCE.XLS and go to the *PROFIT* worksheet.

2) Select cell *B19*, which contains the NPV formula.

3) Select **Tools | Auditing | Trace Precedents**.
   Arrows appear on the worksheet to indicate the cells used as input to the NPV formula.
   The cell range *H2:H13* is surrounded by a border, and a single arrow indicates that the values in all of these cells are used.

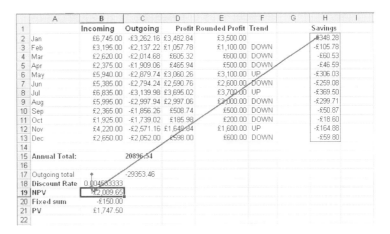

Note: To remove the trace arrows you have added to your worksheet, select **Tools | Auditing | Remove All Arrows**.

Over to you: optional

In this exercise, you will locate precedent cells on other worksheets.

- Select cell *C15* on the *PROFIT* worksheet of MFPF_FINANCE.XLS and trace its precedent cells.
  There are two cells: one on the *INCOMING* worksheet and one on the *OUTGOING* worksheet.

- Double-click the spreadsheet icon at the end of the Precedents arrow and follow the link to one of the precedent cells.

Tracing dependent cells

You could have worked out the precedent cells for any formula by reading the formula. How would you find out whether a particular cell is used by any formula in your spreadsheet, without checking each formula individually?

Excel's **Trace Dependents** command indicates the cells containing formulae that refer to a selected cell.

> **Note: Trace Dependents** will only find dependent cells in worksheets in the same workbook as the selected cell.

In the next exercise, you will trace the dependent cells for one of the monthly profit totals on the *PROFIT* worksheet of MFPF_FINANCE.XLS.

Exercise 18.4: Tracing dependent cells

1) Open MFPF_FINANCE.XLS and go to the *OUTGOING* worksheet.

2) Select cell *B5*.

3) Select **Tools | Auditing | Trace Dependents**.
   Arrows appear on the worksheet to indicate the cells that use cell *B5* as an input.

	A	B	C	D	E	F	G	H	I
1		Warehouse Rental	Electricity	Telephone	Raw Materials	Petrol	Wages	Outgoing total	
2	Jan	-£250.00		-£28.12	-£2,113.00	£3.96	-£875.00	-£3,262.16	
3	Feb	-£250.00	£40.10		-£975.00	£2.88	-£875.00	-£2,137.22	
4	Mar	-£250.00		-£26.50	-£867.50	£4.32	-£875.00	-£2,014.68	
5	Apr	-£250.00	£36.44		-£740.50	£2.00	-£875.00	-£1,909.06	
6	May	-£250.00		-£24.10	-£1,737.00	£6.36	-£875.00	-£2,879.74	
7	Jun	-£250.00	£39.08		-£1,637.00	£6.84	-£875.00	-£2,794.24	
8	Jul	-£250.00		-£28.06	-£1,994.00	£7.08	-£875.00	-£3,139.98	
9	Aug	-£250.00	-£36.34		-£1,842.00	£5.40	-£875.00	-£2,997.94	
10	Sep	-£270.00		-£26.50	-£691.00	£6.24	-£875.00	-£1,856.26	
11	Oct	-£270.00	£36.90		-£558.00	£2.88	-£875.00	-£1,739.02	
12	Nov	-£270.00		-£24.48	-£1,406.00	£4.32	-£875.00	-£2,571.16	
13	Dec	-£270.00	-£37.88		-£872.00	£2.88	-£875.00	-£2,052.00	
14									
15	Annual Total:		-£29,353.46						
16									
17	Outgoing total		-£29,353.46						
18									

> **Note:** Cell *C15* is a dependent of cell *B5*. Cell *C15* is itself a precedent of cell *C15* on the *PROFIT* worksheet. If a dependent cell is itself a precedent cell for the formula in another cell, no arrow appears to indicate this. You will need to check each dependent cell for further dependents.

Chapter summary

Excel allows you to identify the cells in a worksheet that contain formulae by using the **Go To** command, or by switching between displaying formulae and the values they generate.

The **Trace Precedents** command locates all of the cells referred to by the formula in a selected cell, and connects them to the cell containing the formula using arrows.

The **Trace Dependents** command indicates the cells in a workbook containing formulae that refer to a selected cell in the same workbook.

19

Sharing and Protecting your Spreadsheets

In this chapter

There are many reasons you might want to share your spreadsheet with other people: for information purposes only, or so that they can add specific data that you need, for example.

When you give copies of your spreadsheets to other people for information purposes, you may want them to see final values in all of the cells, but not the formulae used to generate them.

If you want someone to add specific data, you might want them to fill in certain values and see a result calculated. You don't want them to change the formulae used, or edit any existing data, you just want them to be able to edit specific cells.

In this chapter, you will look at different ways you can protect all or part of a workbook before sharing it with someone else.

New skills

At the end of this chapter you should be able to:

- Hide and unhide columns and rows in a worksheet
- Hide and unhide worksheets in a workbook
- Protect individual cells in a worksheet
- Apply password protection to worksheets and workbooks

New words

There are no new words in this chapter.

Hiding columns and rows

You can hide individual columns and rows in any Excel worksheet.

After hiding a column or row, you will need to password-protect either the worksheet or the workbook containing the hidden column or row, otherwise anyone can unhide the column or row at any time.

Hiding a column

Joe Molloy from Joe's Hardware lost the books he kept his order records in, so he needs to recreate them. He has asked Mr Murphy for a copy of the delivery records he kept. Mr Murphy has agreed, and asks you to give Joe a copy of the *DELIVERIES* worksheet of DELIVERIES.XLS. Before handing it over, though, you should hide the column that shows the petrol cost for each delivery.

In the next exercise, you will hide column *D* on the *DELIVERIES* worksheet of DELIVERIES.XLS, which shows the cost of petrol for each delivery.

Exercise 19.1: Hiding a column

1) Open DELIVERIES.XLS, and go to the *DELIVERIES* worksheet.

2) Select column *D*.

3) Select **Format | Column | Hide**.
The column disappears.
You can see the location of the hidden column, because the columns in the worksheet now go: *A, B, C, E, F, ...* .

	A	B	C	E
1	DeliveryDate	CompanyName	Delivery charge	
2	Jan-00	Mullens	10	
3	Jan-00	Liam Kinsella and Sons	10	
4	Jan-00	Joe's Hardware	5	

Chapter 19: Sharing and Protecting your Spreadsheets

| *Unhiding a column* | In the next exercise, you will unhide the column you hid in *Exercise 19.1.* |

Exercise 19.2: Unhiding a column

1) Open DELIVERIES.XLS, and go to the *DELIVERIES* worksheet.

2) Select the columns either side of the hidden column, in this case columns *C* and *E*.

3) Select **Format | Column | Unhide**.
   Column *D* reappears.

4) Save and close your workbook when you are done.

Note: If column *A* is hidden, you cannot use the above method to unhide it. Instead, select **Edit | Go To ...** to open the *Go To* dialog box, type *A1* in the *Reference* field, and click **OK**. Then you can select **Format | Column | Unhide** to show the hidden column.

| *Hiding and unhiding rows* | The procedures for hiding and unhiding rows are the same, except that you select the **Row** option on the **Format** menu instead of the **Column** option. |

Hiding worksheets

As well as hiding individual rows and columns in a worksheet, you can select a whole worksheet and hide it from view in your workbook.

Joe Molloy has asked the Murphys to send him his invoices by e-mail in future. They have agreed to send him a copy of the Excel spreadsheet for each invoice.

The invoice template you use, INVOICE_MFPF.XLT, contains two worksheets: *CUSTOMER INVOICE* and *PERSONAL NOTES*. When you pass an invoice on to Joe, you will need to hide the *PERSONAL NOTES* worksheet first.

In the next exercise, you will hide the *PERSONAL NOTES* worksheet of INVOICE1.XLS.

Exercise 19.3: Hiding a worksheet

1) Open INVOICE1.XLS and go to the *PERSONAL NOTES* worksheet.

2) Select **Format | Sheet | Hide**.
   The *PERSONAL NOTES* worksheet disappears.

3) Save the workbook.

You have hidden a whole worksheet in your workbook.

Unhiding worksheets

To unhide worksheets in a workbook, you open a dialog box that lists all of the hidden worksheets in the book, and select the one to unhide.

In the next exercise, you will unhide the worksheet you hid in *Exercise 19.3*.

Exercise 19.4: Unhiding a worksheet

1) Open INVOICE1.XLS.

2) Select **Format | Sheet | Unhide ... .**
   The *Unhide* dialog box appears.

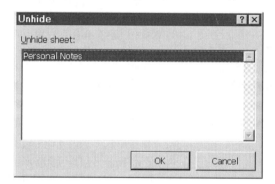

3) The *Unhide* dialog box lists all of the hidden worksheets in the current workbook.
   Select *PERSONAL NOTES* and click **OK**.
   The *PERSONAL NOTES* worksheet reappears.

4) Finally, select **Edit | Repeat Hide** to hide the worksheet again.

   Note: Unless you password-protect your workbook, Joe will be able to unhide the worksheet again just like you did in this exercise. You will learn about password-protecting workbooks in *Protecting workbooks* on page 171.

Chapter 19: Sharing and Protecting your Spreadsheets

Protecting cells

When you share a spreadsheet with other people, you can prevent them from making any changes to it, or you can restrict them to changing only certain cells.

If you are issuing an invoice, you will not want the customer to be able to change any of the details in the invoice. If you are using a spreadsheet as an order form, on the other hand, you will want the customer to be able to enter a quantity for each product, but not change the product list or prices.

You can assign two types of protection to a cell:

- *Locked:* If a cell is locked, you cannot edit the cell's contents.

- *Hidden:* If a cell is hidden, you can see the value in the cell, but if a formula was used to calculate the value, you cannot see the formula.

By default, when you protect a worksheet or workbook, Excel assumes that you want all cells to be locked but not hidden.

> **Note:** The protection setting for a cell is not enforced until you protect the worksheet or workbook containing the cell.

Specifying protection settings for a cell

Joe Molloy has asked you to leave an editable area in the electronic copies of the invoices you send him, where he can enter the date he paid the invoice. Remember, by default all cells will be locked when you password-protect your workbook.

In the next exercise, you will set the protection for a cell on the *CUSTOMER INVOICE* worksheet of INVOICE1.XLS so that Joe can enter into it the date the invoice was paid.

Exercise 19.5: Setting protection for a cell

1) Open INVOICE1.XLS and go to the *CUSTOMER INVOICE* worksheet.

2) In cell *E30*, enter the label *Date paid:*.

3) Select cell *F30*.

4) Select **Format | Cells ... .**
The *Format Cells* dialog box opens.

5) Click the **Protection** tab.

6) Uncheck the checkboxes beside *Locked* and *Hidden*, then click **OK**. Cell *F30* is now unprotected so that even after password protection has been added to the worksheet or workbook, the value in this cell can be edited.

Protecting worksheets

To protect the contents of a worksheet, and to enforce the protection settings applied to cells within it, you will need to protect the sheet itself. You can choose to protect a worksheet with or without a password, but if you do not use a password, then anyone can unprotect the worksheet again.

You can choose to protect one or more of the following:

- *Contents:* If you protect contents in the worksheet, then you cannot edit locked cells and you cannot see the formulae in hidden cells.

- *Objects:* If you protect objects in the worksheet, then embedded objects, for example, graphics, cannot be edited.

- *Scenarios:* If you protect scenarios, then scenario definitions cannot be edited.

In the next exercise, you will protect the contents of the *CUSTOMER INVOICE* worksheet of INVOICE1.XLS.

Exercise 19.6: Protecting a worksheet

1) Open INVOICE1.XLS and go to the *CUSTOMER INVOICE* worksheet.

2) Select **Tools | Protection | Protect Sheet ...** .
The *Protect Sheet* dialog box opens.

3) Check the boxes beside *Contents*.
As there are no objects or scenarios in this workbook, it does not matter whether you check the boxes beside *Objects* and *Scenarios* or leave them unchecked.

4) Enter a password in the *Password* field, and click **OK**.
The *Confirm Password* dialog box opens.

5) Re-enter your password and click **OK**.

You can unprotect the worksheet again at any time by selecting **Tools | Protection | Unprotect sheet** and entering the password you used to protect it.

Protecting workbooks

You can hide or protect individual worksheets in a workbook, but you can still unhide, add and delete worksheets (even protected ones) as long as the workbook itself is unprotected.

You can choose to protect two different aspects of a workbook:

■ *Structure:* If you protect the structure of a workbook, you cannot add, remove, hide or unhide worksheets. Also, you cannot unhide rows or columns, or change the protection on cells or worksheets.

■ *Windows:* If you protect the windows, then the size and location on the screen of the workbook will be the same every time it is opened. You might want to use this setting to resize the Excel window to exactly frame a specific cell range when a workbook is opened.

To make sure that Joe does not unhide the PERSONAL NOTES worksheet, you will protect the workbook containing his invoice.

In the next exercise, you will assign password protection to INVOICE1.XLS, so that no further changes can be made to the workbook.

Exercise 19.7: Protecting a workbook

1) Open INVOICE1.XLS.

2) Select **Tools | Protection | Protect Workbook ...** .
   The *Protect Workbook* dialog box opens.

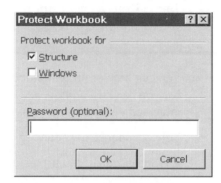

3) Check the checkbox beside *Structure*.

4) Enter a password in the *Password* field and click **OK**.
   The *Confirm Password* dialog box opens.

5) Re-enter your password and click **OK**.

6) Save and close your workbook when you are done.

You can remove the protection again by selecting **Tools | Protection | Unprotect Workbook** and entering the password you used to protect the workbook.

Chapter summary

You can hide individual columns and rows in any Excel worksheet. You can also select a whole worksheet and hide it from view in your workbook.

You can protect any cell against editing, or hide formulae in cells, so that only the final calculated value can be seen.

You can choose to protect data in a worksheet, embedded objects, scenario definitions, or any combination of these three.

You can choose to protect a workbook's structure so that you cannot add, remove, hide or unhide worksheets, unhide rows or columns, or change the protection on cells or worksheets. You can also protect a workbook so that its size and location on the screen of the workbook will be the same every time it is opened.

In conclusion

Now that you have completed all the tasks in this book, you have completed the required syllabus for ECDL Advanced Spreadsheets, and are able to:

- Save time on repetitive tasks by using templates and macros.
- Keep track of the data in your spreadsheets by using named cells and cell ranges, comments and auditing.
- Reuse data by importing them from text files and databases, using different Paste Special options, and creating links between spreadsheets or from Word documents.
- Make your data easier to read by performing multi-column sorts, applying cell and worksheet formatting, customizing charts, and summarizing large amounts of information in PivotTables.
- Use key reference, maths, statistics, database, finance, text, date, time and logical functions.
- Consider how changing the value of a variable will affect your calculations by using data tables and scenarios.
- Protect your work against unauthorized changes by protecting cells, workbooks and worksheets.

Also, thanks to your hard work, the Murphys now have a comprehensive set of spreadsheets that show their sales data for the year, and can track their financial incomings and outgoings. Hopefully, the bank manager will now approve their loan, and, based on the comparative information you have provided, the Murphys will invest wisely for the future.

Congratulations, you have done a great job!

Index

formulae
   cell references in 68
   cells containing 158–9
   custom cell names in 38–9
   display of 159–60
   pasting of 48
   used to link cells 65–7
freezing of row and column titles 74–5
functions
   nesting of 101
   see also database functions; date functions;
      financial functions; logical functions;
      mathematical functions; reference
      func-tions; statistical functions; text
      functions
FV function 128, 148–9

Go To command 158–9
graphics 110–12, 170
groups of objects 61–3

hiding
   of cells 169
   of columns and rows 166–7
   of worksheets 167–8
HLOOKUP function 94–5

IF function 140
import of data 13–28
   from databases 18–21
   from text files 14–18, 21
interest rates, calculations making use of
   128–31
ISERROR function 144

labels 37
linking of cells
   using formulae 65–7
   using Paste Special command 52–3
   to Word documents 68–70
linking of charts 70–1
locked cells 169
logical functions 139–45

Lotus 1-2-3 100, 124
LOWER function 135

macros 81–8
   absolute and relative 83, 85
   assignment to toolbars 86
   disabling of 83
mathematical functions 95–101
mathematical operations using Paste Special
   90
Microsoft Access 120
Microsoft Query 24–8
MONTH function 137

naming of cells and cell ranges 38–9
nesting of functions 101
NPV function 126–7
number formats 77

OR function 23, 25, 142–3

parameters of reference functions 93
passwords 166, 168, 170–2
Paste Link option 52–3
Paste Special command 45–53
   options for 47, 50
   used for mathematical operations 90
   in Word 68
pictures in charts 110–12
pie charts
   changing the angle of slices 112–14
   exploding the slices in 114–15
PivotTables 55–64
   creation of 58–61
   grouping of data in 61–3
   refreshing of 63–4
PMT function 129–30
positive values in cell ranges, summing of
   100
precedent cells 160–1
present values of investments 126–7
PROPER function 134
protection

of cells 169–70
of scenarios 170
of workbooks and worksheets 165–72
   passim
PURECOUNT function 124
PV function 127

qualifiers (of text) 15
queries 18–20, 25 6
   editing of 22
   saving of 21–2
quotation marks
   as qualifiers 15
   for spaces 136
   for strings 134–5

RATE function 131
reference functions 91–4
refreshing of data 4
   in PivotTables 63–4
rounding of numbers 100–1
row titles, freezing of 74–5

saving of queries 21–2
scenarios 152–5
   protection of 170
scrolling 74–5
sharing of spreadsheets 165
Skip blanks option 51–2
sorting 23, 28–35
   by multiple columns 30–1
   order of 31–3
statistical functions 118–20
   see also mathematical functions
strings 134–6

subtotalling 95–7
SUMIF function 98–100, 118
SUMPOSITIVE function 100

templates 5–11
   creation of 9
   creation of spreadsheets from 7–8
   editing of 9–11
text files, import of data from 14–18, 21
text functions 134–6
text qualifiers 15
3D sum function 97–8
TODAY function 136
toolbars, assignment of macros to 86
transposition from row orientation to column
      orientation (and *vice versa*) 52
triangle sign 40
TRUE results 140–4

UPPER function 134

values, pasting of 48
viruses 83
VLOOKUP function 92–4

'What if?' calculations 147
Word documents linked to Excel workbooks
      68–70

.xlt file extension 6

YEAR function 137

zero, division by 51–2